AN INTRODUCTION
TO THE
ABBA SCHOOL

An Introduction
to the
Abba School

Conversations
from the Focolare's
Interdisciplinary Study Center

with contributions by
Chiara Lubich
Piero Coda
Gerard Rosse
Hubertus Blaumeiser
Giuseppe M. Zanghi

introduction by
David L. Schindler

New City Press

Published in the United States of America by
New City Press
202 Cardinal Rd., Hyde Park, NY 12538
©2002 New City Press

Translated by the NCP editorial staff from
Nuova Umanità XIX (1997/1) 109 and XIX (1997/3-4) 111-112
(Lubich), XXI (1999/2) 122 (Coda), XXII (2000/1) 127 (Rosse), XIX
(1997/5) 113 (Blaumeiser), XVIII (1996/1) (Zanghi), XVIII (1996/2)
and XVIII (1996/5) (Lubich)
© Città Nuova, Rome, Italy

ISBN 1-56548-176-3

Cover design by Nick Cianfarani

Printed in Canada

Contents

Introduction

Toward a New Unity of the Disciplines

The key to understanding the significance of the Abba School lies in its conception of "interdisciplinary." Typically today this term refers to a dialogue among the disciplines that presumes an original fragmentation among them. Each discipline gathers evidence in accord with its own methodology, and the contents or conclusions which it derives are then "correlated" more or less externally with those of the other disciplines. Such a dialogue, however, can never result in a genuine integration of thought.

Denying not at all the legitimate autonomy and achievements of the modern disciplines, the Abba School aims for a different sort of disciplinary integration, rooted in a more radical sense of unity. The articles contained in the present volume provide a sustained reflection on the nature of this unity, while pointing toward the new approaches to the disciplines indicated by such a unity.

The integration to be sought, then, comes from the founding core of the Focolare Movement and indeed from the heart of the Gospel itself: what Chiara refers to as the spirituality of unity, centered in Jesus crucified and forsaken. What is this "spirituality of unity," and how can such a "spirituality" dispose and enable us to view differently the contents and methods of intelligence as currently packaged in the modern academic disciplines?

(1) First and above all, the nature of the unity is revealed in Trinitarian love. What this means for Chiara is that each of the divine persons *is* (being) in and through the "non-being" of giving themselves away to each other. The fullness of each person coincides with the "self-emptying" entailed in being *wholly for* the other. The Trinitarian unity embodied in this paradoxical relation of "being" and "non-being" is brought to earth and made possible in the lives of creatures through the Incarnation, and the "new" commandment of Jesus: "As I have loved you, so you also should love one another" (Jn 13:34; 15:12).

The divine Trinitarian love finds its decisive expression in the historical economy in the words of Jesus on the cross: "My God, my God, why have you forsaken me?" (Mk 15:34; Mt 27:46). Chiara describes this forsakenness of Jesus and its importance for unity as follows:

> It is the moment in which he experienced the deepest separation that can ever be imagined. In a certain sense he experiences being separated from his Father with whom he is and remains one. In this way he gives to all people a new unity, even more complete than the one they had lost through sin. He gives them unity with God and among themselves as a participation in his unity with the Father and with us. He is therefore the key to the understanding and accomplishment of unity. (26, below)

Further, Chiara goes on, "in his abandonment Jesus made himself 'sin' (2 Cor 5:21), 'cursed' (Gal 3:13) in order to make himself one with those who were far from God" (27). The comprehensive implications of this abandonment for the problem of unity now come more explicitly into view: *for this reason*, says Chiara—that is, precisely because, in his "abandonment," Jesus makes himself one with those who are or seem furthest from God and most lacking in worth—Jesus crucified and forsaken "really seems to be the God of our times." He is

the divine answer to the abyss of trial and suffering deeply cut into the human heart by the atheism that pervades so much of modern culture; by the poverty of millions of under-privileged; and by the quest for meaning and ideals on the part of the disillusioned and confused new generations.
Jesus forsaken is the God of today also because he is the image of the division that exists between the churches, a division we are more conscious of in our times. (26-27)

Finally, as the "icon and expression of all creation" (28), Mary reveals archetypically for us the creaturely way of Trinitarian-Christological unity. (We can recall here that the Focolare Movement is named the "Work of Mary.") Mary is an integral part of "God's global plan of salvation for all humanity and for the cosmos" (27). Mary's *fiat* ("let it be done unto me according to your Word") enables her "magnification" of the greatness of God and his works. "As she generated the Son of God in the flesh through the work of the Holy Spirit, similarly, having shared in a unique way in the Redemption through her desolation at the foot of the cross (cf. Jn 19: 25-27), she participates efficaciously in the regeneration of the sons and daughters of God brought about by the Holy Spirit in the womb of the Church" (27-28).

Thus we reach the stunning summary breadth and depth of Chiara's sense of unity:

Because there is in God a perfect perichoresis [movement of love] between the three divine Persons, and because, through Christ, in the Spirit, there is also a perichoresis between the Trinity and humanity, apex and synthesis of creation ("You loved them even *as* you loved me" [Jn 17:23]), all creation, recapitulated in Christ, is also destined to be, as Mary already is, eternally set into the Trinity: that is, to live and rejoice infinitely in the intimate life of God, in the ever new and unending dynamism of the Trinitarian relationships. (28)

(2) If we wish to understand properly the interdisciplinary nature of the Abba School, then, we must recognize that the spirituality of unity lying at the heart of the Focolare charism signifies not merely a "moral" or "pious" unity but also and more profoundly a "new" "ontological" unity: it signifies a unity involving the dynamic reordering of all things and all aspects of all things in Jesus forsaken as the ultimate revelation of Trinitarian love. It signifies a change not only in our affective and voluntary attitudes toward God and the world but also and more pertinently in the way we understand the very "logic" of the world itself—of the cosmos in its entirety—as created (and redeemed) by God. Thus Chiara says that when we live in Jesus who is among us, "everything changes, politics and art, education and religion, private life and recreation. Everything" (101). The poem of Chiara concluding the present volume captures the scope of what she intends here:

> I feel in my heart the passion that fills your heart
>   for the forsakenness enveloping the whole world
> I love everyone who is sick and lonely:
> I even feel for plants that are in distress,
> and for animals that are left alone.
> Who will console their weeping? . . . .
> Let me be in this world, my God, the tangible sacrament
>   of your love, of your being Love:
> Let me be the arms to embrace and transform into love all
>   the loneliness of the world. (106)

Though the vision is put poetically here, it is essential, once again, not to attenuate its ontological meaning. Human beings are to be the "sacrament" of God's love, which is to say, in light of the work of the Abba School, they are to recapitulate the *order* of creaturely things, of all things, human and non-human, in terms finally of the meaning-unity revealed in Jesus forsaken. This meaning-unity is not something foreign to things, hence something to be (arbitrarily) imposed on them. On the contrary, it is their most original and ultimate truth as creatures. Thus the task of recapitulation involves a "new" theology and philosophy and anthropology; but it also involves a "new" cosmology and indeed a "new" way of conceiving the human and natural sciences. The present book contains sustained reflections on the new theology and philosophy carried in the charism of unity, while pointing a direction for the new cosmology and for the various disciplines represented by the twenty-five scholars currently making up the Abba School.

We might sum up this direction, in a word, by saying that it involves developing a "new" notion of being, ordered from and toward the Beatitudes, which "depict the countenance of Jesus Christ and portray his charity."[1] It consists in rethinking all of reality in terms of the "transcendentals"—unity, beauty, goodness, truth—now recapitulated in terms of the love expressed in the Beatitudes. It entails a recovery of things in their inherent meaning and attractiveness and worth, hence also in their original "uselessness" and indeed vulnerability; a recovery of things in the generosity that signifies the original and most basic meaning of their "power" (e.g., causal agency).

Thus the fundamental question generated in and by the Abba School is how this new vision can acknowledge and appropriate all that is true and good and beautiful in the presently-configured disciplines, while at the same time transforming the content and methods of these disciplines in the light of the ultimate unity of things as revealed in the loving "power"/"powerlessness" of God in Jesus. It goes without saying that the rethinking indicated here is not a matter of "softness" or "vagueness" but of the utmost rigor and precision: a rigor and a precision that, nonetheless, are those proper to a lover, not a machine. It is a matter of deepening, not short-circuiting, the inner dynamics of intelligence, integrated now into the order of holiness.

(3) All of the foregoing, however, remains unsettled until we face the persistent question of "realism." Even—indeed precisely—if we grant the truth of Chiara's vision of unity in all its radicality, what realistic hope can there be of

"implementing" it—practically, effectively—in today's world? Precisely *because* the modern world is so pervasively ordered by a power contrary to that affirmed in the Beatitudes, how can we really view the proposal of Jesus forsaken as anything other than naive and romantic—indeed utopian?

The meaning of "realism" must of course turn finally on what it means to be (real). And Chiara's insistence, following the Gospel, is that the meaning of being is most truly exhibited in the paradoxical unity of being and non-being: in love. But, with this assertion, we have not yet met the full burden of the objection, for this "real" meaning of being as love is at the same time, not only in the modern world but also in the entire infralapsarian condition of humankind, also "ideal": its very here-and-now reality as love is also and intrinsically (in the one historical order) a reality-yet-to-come. In addressing the question of realism, in other words, we have to come to terms with the abiding tension between "real" and "ideal" that is implied in Chiara's own appeal to the Gospel.

I note all of this for two reasons. First, anyone who invokes the issue of utopianism must him or her self come to terms with what he or she is inevitably presupposing about the nature of the "real," and indeed about the sense in which the "ideal" is both already present and yet to come. Secondly, it is of the essence of Chiara's vision to insist that it is Jesus himself who finally discloses the nature of the "real" and indeed of the relation between the "ideal" and the "real." It is precisely Jesus in our midst—incarnate, forsaken, resurrected—who reveals the ultimate, deepest, and most proper meaning of "realism": reveals both its truth and its way. Let us conclude with comments on each of these two points.

First, philosopher Alasdair MacIntyre, responding to the charge of utopianism made against his own proposals regarding the modern liberal university, illustrates well—and with customary trenchancy—how such a charge always carries its own (often unconscious, hence question-begging) assumptions:

Those most prone to accuse others of utopianism are generally those men and women of affairs who pride themselves upon their pragmatic realism, who look for immediate results, who want the relationship between present input and future output to be predictable and measurable, and that is to say, a matter of the shorter, indeed the shortest run. They are the enemies of the incalculable, the skeptics about all expectations which outrun what *they* take to be hard evidence, the deliberately shortsighted who congratulate themselves upon the limits of their vision. Who were their predecessors?

They include the fourth-century magistrates of the types of disordered city which Plato described in Book VIII of the *Republic*, the officials who tried to sustain the pagan Roman Empire in the age of Augustine, the sixteenth-century protobureaucrats who continued obediently to do the unprincipled bidding of Henry VIII while Thomas More set out on the course that led to his martyrdom. What these examples suggest is that the gap between Utopia and current social reality may on occasion furnish a measure, not of the lack of justification of Utopia, but rather of the degree to which those who not only inhabit contemporary social reality but insist upon seeing only what it allows them to see and upon learning only what it allows them to learn, cannot even identify, let alone confront, the problems which will be inscribed in their epitaphs. It may be therefore that the charge of utopianism is sometimes best understood more as a symptom of the condition of those who level it than an indictment of the projects against which it is directed.[2]

What MacIntyre thus makes clear is that the conventional charge of unrealism or utopianism presupposes just the instrumentalized and fragmentary mode of rationality, the very notions of practice and practical, of "ideal" and "real," which a vision of unity such as that of the Abba School means to call into question.

Secondly, the very method of the Abba School that calls these conventional notions into question itself witnesses to the depth and seriousness of what is implied in the charge of "unrealism." The very method of the Abba School, in other words, testifies to how we must resist assuming that the response needed to the problems of our time can be realized easily or quickly—for example, through management techniques or political strategies or "expert" analyses. The needed response, on the contrary, requires just the sort of method that the School itself has followed since its inception some fifty years ago: namely, a reflection sustained by and centered in a life of community and entailing a transformation of one's being and consciousness through prayer, the suffering of differences, and the like, all of which presuppose the duration of time.

In a word, the Abba School in its own history discloses the method that alone, finally, bears the capacity to address truly the problems of our time: a method summed up in what may be termed the ontological patience of Jesus—and Mary— from whom we learn that there is no resurrection, or final realization of truth, goodness, and beauty, except in and through abiding disponibility (*fiat*), incarnation, (eventual) abandonment, crucifixion, and death. It is in the light of these alone that we discover the ultimate, and finally only pertinent, meaning of "realism."

Theologian Hans Urs von Balthasar held that the most fundamental problem of our age, the problem lying within and most profoundly defining the entire range of problems peculiar to modern culture, originates in the centuries-old tendency in the West to separate intelligence—the contents and methods of our knowledge of the cosmos—from the order of holiness. If this is accurate, as I believe it to be, then we are right to conclude that the Abba School, which is dedicated to the integration of intelligence and holiness in and through Jesus forsaken, is one of the truly significant developments of our time, both in the Church and for the broader culture.

David L. Schindler
Washington, D.C.

Notes

1. *Catechism of the Catholic Church*, 1717.
2. Alasdair MacIntyre, *Three Rival Versions of Moral Enquiry* (Notre Dame, IN: University of Notre Dame Press, 1990), 234-235.

David L. Schindler is Editor of the North American edition of *Communio* and Dean and Gagnon Professor of Fundamental Theology at the John Paul II Institute for Studies on Marriage and Family at The Catholic University of America.

Editorial Preface

The beginning of Chiara Lubich's journey with the Focolare Movement she founded was marked by a period of intense illumination, analogies of which can be found in the history of some of the great charisms and spiritual movements that have risen up in the Church throughout the centuries.

The first few years of the Focolare were characterized by a new discovery of the gospel; Chiara with a group of friends strove to live its every word with renewed determination. Due to the rapid expansion of the Movement, they were very intense years for Chiara, so much so that in early 1949 she was advised to take time off to rest. Thus, with some of her friends she left Rome for the Dolomite Mountains in northern Italy. Soon, Igino Giordani, a highly renowned politician, journalist, and scholar, joined them. His arrival marked the beginning of a period of special graces that are now the object of study of an interdisciplinary study group called "Abba School." Its aim is to unfold the doctrine and the potential contribution to contemporary culture implicit in the Focolare's spirituality.

Today, the Abba School is made up of twenty-five scholars of various disciplines, ranging from the humanities to the sciences. They meet regularly with Chiara at the Movement's headquarters near Rome. Through their work a new unity is emerging between the various disciplines with theology and among themselves.

The articles printed here, previously published in *Nuova Umanità*, a periodical of modern cultural thought, represent the first-fruits of this study. The printing of the present volume grew from a desire to offer a more complete presentation, at least for the time being, of the contents of this study and of the unique methodology of the school's scholars.

We hope that through an attentive and meditative reading of the present collection the reader might intuit the beginnings of a doctrine that can give new light to the various human sciences.

Please note: All the quotations from Chiara Lubich's writings printed in the articles to follow are taken from unpublished works and are therefore reported here without a citation.

Toward a Theology and Philosophy of Unity

The Principal Cornerstones

The first article of this present collection is compiled from the acceptance speeches of Chiara Lubich, foundress of the Focolare Movement, on being awarded honorary degrees in theology and philosophy (respectively at St. Thomas University, Manila, and Jean Baptiste de la Salle University, Mexico City, in January and June 1997).

To begin quite simply, when I was young my ideal was to study, especially to study philosophy. In my search for truth, what satisfied my mind and heart most fully was studying the ancient and the modern philosophers.

Since I had been raised a Christian, however, I soon realized, perhaps through an impulse of the Holy Spirit, that my deepest interest was centered on one thing alone: to get to know God.

I thought, therefore, that my strong desire to know God would be satisfied if I could attend the Catholic University. Because my family's financial situation was precarious, I was unable to pursue this option. Even though I applied for the limited number of scholarships available to young women, I was not awarded one. When I found out I was deeply disappointed. I was desolate and I cried my heart out. While my mother was trying to console me, something rather unusual occurred. From within I seemed to hear a subtle voice suggesting, "I will be your teacher!" and I immediately felt at peace.

I was a Catholic and went to communion every day. One day I understood something new; it was like a light.

I questioned myself: So you think you are looking for the truth? Isn't there someone who said that he personally is the truth? Didn't Jesus say, "I am the truth"?

This was one of the main reasons that prompted me to seek the truth not so much in books but in Jesus. And I resolved to follow him.

Meanwhile, this was 1943, Providence was giving life to what would eventually become the Focolare Movement. I was continuing my studies at a state university, but due to the increasing demands of the newly-born Movement, I had to interrupt my studies and then start them again. I did this four-teen times. Then one day I put my beloved books in the attic once and for all.

One book, however, I kept: the Gospels.

Since the war was raging I would take that book with me when my friends and I fled to the air-raid shelters. There we would read it. We were astonished: the words we had read so many times before took on a profound meaning, a singular beauty; they shone out as if there were a light beneath them. They were different from all other words, even from the ones we found in the best spiritual books. They were universal words and therefore suited to everyone: youth, adults, men, women, Italians, Koreans, Ecuadorians, Nigerians. . . . They were eternal words, for every age, therefore also for ours. And they could be put into practice. They were written with divine artistry. They impelled people to translate them into life.

Keypoints of the spirituality of unity

While the entire Gospel attracted us, to the point that we considered it to be the rule of the newly-born Movement, a light (now we can say, a charism) lead us to emphasize certain words, and we made them our own. Those words, like rings in a chain, would become the key ideas of a new spirituality of the Church: the spirituality of unity.

These key ideas were:
- God, the new ideal of our life, who in the midst of the horrors of the war, the fruit of hatred, manifested himself for what he truly is: Love.
- Doing God's will and living his word as our possibility to respond to his love with our love.
- Love of neighbor, especially of the needy, as the commandment that sums up all the law and the prophets.
- Carrying out this love, reciprocally and radically, by living Jesus' characteristic new commandment.
- Consequently, accomplishing unity with him and with our brothers and sisters, as it is understood from his prayer for unity.
- Living with the presence of Jesus among us, as he promised to those, even two or three, who are united in his name, that is, in his love.
- Loving the cross, fixing our gaze on Jesus crucified in his terrible abandonment, which we discovered—as I will illustrate later—as the key to unity.

Moreover, this included nourishing ourselves daily with the eucharist, the bond of unity; living the Church, especially as "communion"; imitating Mary, "Mother of unity," in her desolation; allowing ourselves to be guided by the Holy Spirit, Love personified in the Trinity and bond of unity also among the members of the mystical Body of Christ.

A communitarian spirituality

This decision of ours would eventually bring about in the Church, perhaps for the first time, a spirituality that proved to be, upon studying it, more communitarian than individual; that is, a spirituality that allows not only the individual person, but many, indeed, very many, to reach perfection.

And it was a kind of holiness—as we are still discovering—surprisingly suited to our times.

We were always aware and convinced that what comes to life in the Church must be in full communion with its Magisterium. A couple of decades after the Focolare's birth, in the 1970's, we wanted to compare the main points of our spirituality, as they were understood and lived, with what had been said by the Fathers of the Church, the Ecumenical Councils, the saints, popes and great theologians.

We rejoiced to see the incredible consonance which confirmed that we were one with our mother the Church, although in our own specific way of thinking and acting.

This resulted in a deeper, more enlightened understanding of the Church's entire doctrine; steeping ourselves in it, each one of us was helped to be formed more and more, we hoped, as "Church-souls."

Doctrine

Lately we have come to realize that from this new life, from this experience of ours, a particular doctrine is coming forth. This doctrine is anchored to the eternal truth of Revelation and develops and renews the theological tradition.

On the other hand, it is not the first time that something like this has happened in the Church. Didn't the Spirit draw out a new doctrine from the experience of Francis, entrusting this task specifically to Bonaventure, Duns Scotus, and others? And isn't Thomas Aquinas the theologian of the Order founded by Dominic besides being the "doctor *communis*"?

Likewise, we too, after almost fifty years of life saw a similar possibility arising (although it is not so much us but God who is at work).

The presence in the Movement of Bishop Klaus Hemmerle, a well-known, profound and modern German theologian and philosopher, now deceased, and of men and women Focolarini scholars, offered the occasion to open a center that would study this doctrine: the so-called Abba School.

In it, among other things, we also study intuitions or illuminations covering the vast range of our faith which it seems the Spirit suggested to us, especially in 1949, a time close to the beginning of our Movement.

And, thanks to God, when we study with the presence of Jesus among us, as is characteristic of the Focolare, we often find ourselves immersed in a light from above, as it were, an expression, we believe, of that Wisdom for which Jesus thanked the Father for having hidden from the wise and the learned and revealed to the little ones.

The Charism of Unity and Theology

It is a new theology springing forth from the life of the charism of unity and, at the same time, a new philosophy. What are the principal cornerstones of the theology that is emerging from the charism of unity? I would like to describe some of them here, although these are certainly not the only areas of study and research being undertaken. They are: God who is Love, unity, Jesus crucified and forsaken, and Mary.

God who is Love

Yes, first of all, God who is Love. What John Paul II said of the spirituality given to us by God holds true for our theology as well, namely, that its first inspiring spark was love.[1]

Clearly, it is not just any kind of love, but *agape*, the love of God, the Love that *is* God. The departure point of our experience and of the theology that emerges from it is, therefore, the same as that of Christian faith itself: "We have come to know and to believe in the love God has for us. God is Love" (1 Jn 4:16).

The originality of Christian revelation, which opens up the unprecedented depths of God's self-revelation in the Old Testament, "I Am who Am" (Ex 3:14), at the same time bringing to unexpected fruition the seeds of the Word dispersed in the various religions, is contained in this New Testament confession of faith: "God is Love."

Love, therefore, is not only an attribute of God; it is his very Being. And because he is Love, God is One and Triune at the same time: Father, Son and Holy Spirit.

Jesus—above all in the Paschal event of his passion, in which he was driven to annihilation through his abandonment and death, which results in his Resurrection and the effusion of the Spirit—reveals to us the Being of the Trinity as Love.

The Father generates the Son out of love, he loses himself in the Son, he lives in him; in a certain sense he makes himself "non-being" out of love, and for this very reason, he *is*, he is the Father. The Son, as echo of the Father, out of love turns to him, he loses himself in the Father, he lives in him, and in a certain sense he makes himself "non-being" out of love; and for this very reason, he *is*, he is the Son. The Holy Spirit, since he is the mutual love between the Father and the Son, their bond of unity, in a certain sense he also makes himself "non-being" out of love, and for this very reason, he *is*, he is the Holy Spirit.

Unity, the model of the Trinitarian life

Closely linked to this first cornerstone is the second: unity.

As I said earlier, from the very beginning of the Movement we were overpowered by the words of Jesus' prayer for unity:

"As you, Father, are in me and I in you, that they also may be in us, that the world may believe that you sent me" (Jn 17:21).

Seeking to put these words into practice, we discovered a light pouring out from them that illuminated God's design of love for humanity.

We understood that Jesus is the Word of God made man in order to teach men and women to live according to the model of the life of the Trinity, that life which he lives in the bosom of the Father.

He did not stop at pointing out and closely connecting the two central commandments of the Old Testament: "You shall love the Lord, your God, with all your heart, with all your soul, and with all your mind. . . . You shall love your neighbor as yourself" (Mt 22:37-39). He taught us the commandment that he himself does not hesitate to describe as "my commandment" and "new," with which it is possible to live the Trinitarian life on earth: "As I have loved you, so you also should love one another" (Jn 13:34; 15:12).

The commandment of mutual love lived out and measured against Jesus' love for us, to the point of the abandonment that consumes us into one in him, defines the heart of Christian anthropology—as the Second Vatican Council under-lined[2]—the vision of the human person revealed to us by Jesus.

When we live the new commandment, seeking to receive the gift of unity in Jesus that comes to us from the Father, the life of the Trinity is no longer lived only in the interior life of the individual person, but it flows freely among the members of the Mystical Body of Christ.

Thus the mystical body of Christ can now be brought to that fullness already made possible in the grace of faith and the sacraments, especially the eucharist: the presence of the risen Christ in history, who lives again in each one of his disciples and in their midst (cf. Mt 18:20).

Jesus crucified and forsaken

And now the third cornerstone: Jesus crucified and forsaken.

The Holy Spirit, we believe, even before making us penetrate the mystery of unity, focused our faith and our exclusive love on Jesus who cried out from the cross, as I said before, in a climax of love and suffering, "My God, my God, why have you forsaken me?" (Mk 15:34; Mt 27:46).

It is the moment in which he experiences the deepest separation that can ever be imagined. In a certain sense he experiences being separated from his Father with whom he is and remains one. In this way he gives to all people a new unity, even more complete than the one they had lost through sin. He gives them unity with God and among themselves as a participation in his unity with the Father and with us. He is therefore the key to the understanding and the accomplishment of unity.

In order to achieve unity, it is really necessary to keep present and to love Jesus forsaken (this was how we called Jesus in this mystery that summarizes and is central to his redemptive mission); it is necessary to love him in a radical way, as Paul did: "I resolved to know nothing while I was with you except Jesus Christ, and him crucified" (1 Cor 2:2).

Furthermore, as scripture says, in his abandonment Jesus made himself "sin" (2 Cor 5:21), "cursed" (Gal 3:13) in order to make himself one with those who were far from God.

For this reason, Jesus crucified and forsaken really seems to be the God of our times: the divine answer to the abyss of trial and suffering deeply cut into the human heart by the atheism that pervades so much of modern culture; by the poverty of millions of deprived people; and by the quest for meaning and ideals by the disillusioned and confused new generations.

Jesus forsaken is the God of today also because he is the image of the divisions that exist between Christian churches,

divisions we are more conscious of in our times. Discovering ?
his countenance in these divisions is precisely what gives us
hope to be able to cooperate in an effective and vital way in the
process of reunification.

In particular, we seem to understand that in him "who was
God and emptied himself"—as Paul writes in his letter to the
Philippians (2:6-7)—a providential way is opening for
dialogue with the faithful of the religious traditions of the ?
East, and this represents one of the most demanding and
urgent frontiers at the dawning of the third millennium.

Mary

Finally, Mary. We feel that she cannot be merely one theme
among others of our theology, important as they may be.
Perhaps because ours is her Work, the Work of Mary; perhaps
because today many signs of the times and authoritative words
of the Magisterium speak to us of the emerging "Marian
profile" of the Church; perhaps because we witness the
singular phenomenon of the figure of Mary being recognized
by other religious faiths, we can see the heralding of a new and
original season of Mariological reflection.

In such reflection, we believe, the reality of Mary needs to
be explored in the context of God's global plan of salvation for
all humanity and for the cosmos.

In fact, as John Paul II said recently, Mary is "an integral
part of the economy of communicating the Trinity to the
human race."[3] She is the Mother of the Word of God made
man, which places her in an extraordinary and unique relationship with all the persons of the Most Holy Trinity (cf. Lk
1:35). This, above all, is the real greatness of Mary, which
"magnifies" the greatness of God and his works.

But Mary is also Mother of the Church. As she generated
the Son of God in the flesh through the work of the Holy
Spirit, similarly, having shared in a unique way in the
redemption through her desolation at the foot of the cross (cf.

Jn 19:25-27), she participates efficaciously in the regeneration of the sons and daughters of God brought about by the Holy Spirit in the womb of the Church.

Mary, now in heaven, God's design for her completely fulfilled, is the flower and first fruit of the Church and of creation, which in her is already Christified, divinized. In a certain way, we can think of her as being set into the Trinity, through grace, as icon and expression of all creation.

Because there is in God a perfect *perichoresis*[4] between the three divine Persons, and because, through Christ, in the Spirit, there is also a *perichoresis* between the Trinity and humanity, which is the apex and synthesis of creation ("You loved them even *as* you loved me" [Jn 17:23]), all creation, recapitulated in Christ, is also destined to be, as Mary already is, eternally set into the Trinity: that is, to live and rejoice infinitely in the intimate life of God, in the ever-new and unending dynamism of the Trinitarian relationships.

The center of revelation

As can be understood from what I have said, the doctrine that springs forth from this charism of unity gives the impression of peering into the center of revelation.

Our theologians, in fact, quoting von Balthasar, recall that "Charisms like those of Augustine, Francis, Ignatius, can receive, as gifts from the Spirit, *glimpses into the center of revelation*, glimpses that enrich the Church in a very unexpected and yet everlasting way. They are always," continues the great theologian, "charisms in which intelligence, love and discipleship are inseparable. This shows that the Spirit is at once divine wisdom and divine love, and in no case pure theory, but always living practice."[5]

Above all, these professors point out that those who deepen their understanding of this doctrine—because they try to live in accordance with this charism of unity, remaining united in the name of Jesus so that he is present among them, and nourishing themselves daily with Jesus in the eucharist—can in a special way participate in his life or, as Augustine says,[6] be made one with him.

Therefore, an innovation that seems to emerge from the charism lived in this way is that the theology which results here is not only a theology *about* Jesus but a theology *of* Jesus: of Jesus present in and among theologians.

They observe, in fact, that the predominant method followed in Christian reflection has been that of looking to Jesus above all as the *object* of theology. Obviously, there always was the awareness that such an object—the Son of God made man—required an adequate knowing subject, that is, reason illuminated by faith, a Christified reason.

Nonetheless, with the exception, we believe, of the works of theologians who were also charismatics and often saints . . . generally, theology in the West, especially in the recent past, has been more of a reflection on God and on Jesus, a knowledge, therefore, almost "from without," rather than from within the mystery being considered through participating, with faith and love, in the knowledge that Jesus has of the Father. "No one knows the Son," said Jesus, "except the Father, and no one knows the Father except the Son and anyone to whom the Son wishes to reveal him" (Mt 11:27).

And this is a knowledge that is given by Jesus, through his Spirit, to his mystical body, and that is fully received when we are "one" in him (cf. Gal 3:28), almost one "*mystica persona.*"[7]

A theology of Jesus

Thus, through this charism of unity, the necessary condition is present for the rebirth of a great theology *of* Jesus—clearly, not the Jesus of two thousand years ago, but the Jesus who lives today in the Church.

This leads to a second innovation. Since this theology is the theology "of" Jesus who ascended *into the bosom of the Father*, who lives today in the unity which is the Church, it would be characterized by a certain perspective: from the point of unity, from the One, that is, from God, in whom everything is in its true reality.

Therefore, it would be "one" perspective, next to others, which would not exclude the others; on the contrary, it would presuppose and give value to them. At the same time, it could also offer an original contribution, that of harmonizing them, because it could lead them to unity, illuminating them through a new horizon.

Furthermore, since in a certain sense, as we already mentioned, it is a theology of Jesus, in whom all created realities are recapitulated, it would shed light also on the various sciences, making them truer, more authentic.

Indeed, we can dream that theology would return to being the mother of the other sciences and, why not, even the queen, although in a different sense from that intended in the Middle Ages, not destroying their legitimate autonomy, but leading them back to their true root and their true end.

The Charism of Unity and Philosophy

There is also a new philosophy emerging from the charism of unity. Philosophy is known as the science of the "whys" in the sense that it seeks to explore in-depth the questions posed by men and women and, as much as possible, to give an answer to them.

After decades of intense spiritual life in line with this new spirituality, we realized that there is a moment in the life of Jesus that is pregnant with answers to all our questions.

It is the moment of that great, very great "why" that Jesus addressed to God before dying, his mysterious cry: "My God, my God, why have you forsaken me?" (Mt 27:46).

Jesus forsaken: the God for today

Initially, however, when we decided to follow him in this way, we didn't feel prompted so much to meditate or to formulate the doctrine that might lie beneath his abandonment. Instead, we immediately discovered Jesus forsaken as the key to re-composing unity.

Placing Jesus forsaken as the ideal of our life gave us the courage to run there where he is most present and, by loving him, by taking him into ourselves, work to relieve sufferings and to build unity.

But, as I said before, Jesus forsaken did not present himself to us only as the answer to the existential questions of humanity. He—God who asks God "why," wants a reason for the severed relationship that seems to touch the very unity of God!—is certainly *the* question, so to speak, pushed to its deepest, most radical expression, to where no human question dares to go. Thus, he seems to be the one who best represents human intelligence in the face of mystery.

At the same time, he asks his great "why" precisely in order to give the answer to the many "whys" that are more the object of philosophical reflection, as the Abba School seeks to illustrate.

I will give two examples of this reflection, briefly and simply.

The mystery of being

Let us begin with the first: the mystery of *being*.

What answer does Jesus forsaken give us?

However one may define it in the language of different cultures, the fundamental affirmation of human thought is: being *is*. It is the acknowledgment of that great ocean of existence that human beings are immersed in along with everyone and everything.

This is the most simple, single, and primordial certainty; from this we can then proceed to penetrate the multiple and complex levels of reality.

Everything can be negated, but being cannot.

Being is presented to us by all that is around us (the variety of real things) and within us (our inner lives).

The existence of the smallest things as of the greatest expresses with all its reality: being *is*.

This being—which is common to all realities and through which they are not a non-entity—reveals, in a natural manifestation, *that* Being which none of them is, but which is proclaimed by all. Their becoming, their limits, the very cessation of existence is the language which states that the being of all that exists is rooted in a Being that simply and absolutely *is*.

Referring to the sun, Francis said, with the language of a poet and the profundity of a mystic: "And he heralds You, his Most High Lord."[8]

We can say the same thing for our inner lives. The awareness human beings have had of themselves from the very beginnings of philosophical reflection, especially if enlightened by faith, is the acknowledgment of being. This awareness is a light and, at the same time, a confession of the Absolute Being, of the most pure Light which knows neither shadow nor error. The very light that shines forth in the consciousness of human beings invokes and seeks this most pure Light as its guarantee, its certainty, and its final destination.

So for human beings to say "I" is equivalent to opening themselves to say, in communion with the being of all things, that the Absolute Being *is*.

And yet, the course of philosophy in the West has seen the blurring of these initial certitudes. Self-awareness has been—and is—lived in opposition to the objectivity of being. And it has closed itself to the Absolute Being.

This has led to the great crisis that has marked recent centuries.

Now we could ask ourselves: is it really true that self-awareness and being—as the affirmation of reality in itself to the point of acknowledging the Absolute Being—cannot co-exist?

Or rather, are we not called by this very crisis to examine in depth both the concept of the conscious subject and that of being in all its breadth? And in this way to understand that the challenge today lies ultimately in calling for a new, more fully developed solution, in which the Christian charism shines forth in all its power?

Jesus forsaken is the master of light, of thought, and also (I dare say) of philosophy, precisely on this point.

There may be those who think that to affirm self is to struggle against all that is not self, because what is not self is perceived as a limit and, what is more, as a threat to the integrity of self. But Jesus forsaken, in that terrible moment of his passion, tells us that while the awareness of his subjectivity appears to be diminishing because it seems he is being annulled, in that very moment it *is* in all its fullness.

He shows us, by his being reduced to nothing, accepted out of love for the Father to whom he re-abandons himself ("Into your hands I commend my spirit," Lk 23:46), that I am myself, not when I close myself off from the other, but when I give myself, when out of love I am lost in the other. If, for example, I have a flower and I give it away, certainly I deprive myself of it, and in depriving myself I am losing something of myself (this is non-being); in reality, because I give that flower, love grows in me (this is being). Therefore, my subjectivity *is* when it *is not out of love*, that is, when it is completely transferred, out of love, into the other.

Jesus forsaken is the greatest revelation of how self-awareness can become self-affirmation, for in the very moment that he gives himself to the other, he gives himself to otherness which, stretched to its greatest range, in fact, is being. Authentic self-awareness is that which is born from communion with being, a communion in which awareness seems to lose itself but, in reality, it finds itself, it *is*.

Jesus forsaken thus enlightens being, revealing it as love. And with this he reveals to us that the Absolute Being itself is Love, as affirmed in the first letter of John.

It is so in the dynamic relationship of the three divine Persons, One with the Other, One for the Other, One in the Other.

There are three Persons in the most holy Trinity, and yet they are One because Love *is not* and *is* at the same time.

In the relationship of the three divine Persons, each one, being Love, *is* completely by *not being*, each one mutually indwelling in an eternal self-giving.

In the light of the Trinity, Being reveals itself, if we can say this, as safekeeping in its most inner recesses the non-being of Self-giving: not the non-being that negates Being, but the non-being that reveals Being as Love: *Being which is the three divine Persons.*

In the light of Jesus forsaken, the subject, the being of all created things, and the Absolute Being itself, find therefore a new explanation that can establish a new philosophy of being.

This was the hope of great thinkers of our times, like Maritain and Przywara, who glimpsed the possibility of progressing in the quest for truth precisely on the basis of understanding being as love, as it shines out from the cross of Christ.[9]

Creation

A second point I would like to touch on concerns the significance of creation.

The Hebrew-Christian revelation looks at the world as a creation of God, of a personal God. It is destined, therefore, to have a lasting relationship with him.

Thus, the world has a value in itself as well as its own autonomy, which is actualized in history, in that personal entity that is the human person, endowed with the gift of dialoging directly with God and with other human beings.

Furthermore, the world finds its eschatalogical fulfillment in the Person of the Word incarnate and risen, the only You of the Father, who recapitulates all in himself.

According to Revelation, then, the world is seen as being filled with the presence of God in his Word, through the Spirit. In the history of the West, this Christian view of the world gradually replaced the mythological vision of it, but in the process it was marked by a cultural crisis that, in our times, has given rise to various phenomena such as secularization, secularism, and post- modernity.

Consequently, it is no longer understood how God can fill the world with himself.

Thus, for Western people the world has gradually become empty of meaning. The same goes, according to some schools of thought, for time and history.

A skeptical and cold rationality, dealing with things without penetrating them to their original depth, has replaced the loving understanding that was capable, rather, of grasping the truth and beauty of creation at its roots, that is, in God who contains creation within himself and nurtures it with himself.

The groaning of creation of which Paul speaks (see Rm 8:22), seems no longer to be heard, covered as it is by what Heidegger called the "empty babbling of existence," and therefore of an "inauthentic" culture.[10]

Are we facing an irreversible crisis?

Or, rather, the slow coming to birth of a new world?

Here, too, Jesus forsaken provides a light for understanding and living the meaning of this drama.

Jesus forsaken took upon himself and experienced personally the non-being of creatures separated from the source of being: he took upon himself the "vanity of vanities" (Qo 1:2).

Out of love, he made his own this non-being that we can call negative, transforming it into himself, into that positive non-being which is Love, as the resurrection reveals. Jesus forsaken made the Holy Spirit overflow onto creation, thus becoming "mother" of the new creation.

Certainly, this event is still in gestation: but in the risen Christ, and in Mary assumed into heaven with him, it is already accomplished and, in a way, it is already a reality for his mystical Body, which is the Church.

If we live in mutual love, which brings Christ among us, and if we nourish ourselves with the eucharist, which makes us become Christ as individuals and as a community and, therefore, Church, we can grasp and perceive the penetration of the Spirit of God in the heart of all beings, in each one and in the entire universe. And through the Holy Spirit we intuit the existence of a spousal relationship between the Uncreated and creation, because by becoming flesh, the Word aligned himself with creation thereby divinizing it and recapitulating it in himself.

This wide and majestic vision makes us think of the entrance of all creation one day into the bosom of the Father.

And we can already see signs of this.

For example, at death we consign our body to the earth. Can we not see the body, nourished as it was with the eucharist and therefore Christified, as eucharist for nature? Thus in the heart of the earth, although our flesh would appear to be transformed into earth, in reality it is mysteriously at work as a seed for transfiguring the universe into "the new heavens and the new earth" (Is 66:22; 2 Pt 3:13).

Certainly, these new heavens and the new earth are still far from their full realization, but we can already see them developing in the heart of creation if we look at it with the eyes of the Risen One who lives in us and among us.

This puts everything in a new light and broadens the relationship between people and the world. The capacity to transform things through work and technology is only one aspect of this relationship.

It seems to us that we can say, because of the experience we have had, that the most profound intuitions—whether in the world of ideas, art, science, or works—if they stem from unity among us, unity through which we obtain the presence of the

Risen One among us and participate in his thought (see 1 Cor 2:16), can give us an insight into this strong presence of the Spirit of God in all things. . . .

Your Excellencies, Ladies and Gentlemen.

These are a few words concerning my passionate concern for Jesus, Word of the Father, and how he, especially in his abandonment, can be a light for all of us.

Chiara Lubich

Notes

1. Visit of John Paul II to the Focolare's international headquarters, Rocca di Papa (Rome), August 19, 1984; cf. *Città Nuova*, #17, 1984.

2. Cf. *Gaudium et spes*, 22, 24.

3. John Paul II, "Mary's Relationship with the Trinity," in *L'Osservatore Romano*, Weekly English Edition, #3, January 17, 1996, p. 11.

4. *Perichoresis*: the movement of love among the persons of the Trinity.

5. *Teologica* III, Jaca Book, Milan 1992, p. 22.

6. Augustine, *In Jo. Ev.*, tract. 21:8-9: PL 35, 1568-69.

7. Thomas Aquinas, *De ver.* 29, 7 ad 11.

8. "Canticle of the Sun." in *Francis* by Murray Bodo, St. Anthony Messenger Press, 1972, p. 174.

9. See J. Maritain, *Breve trattato dell'esistenza e dell'esistente*, Brescia 1965, p. 66. E. Przywara, *Filosofia e Teologia dell'Occidente*, Rome 1970, pp. 55-59.

10. See M. Heidegger, *Essere e tempo*, Milan, 1982, cited in G. Reale and D. Antiseri, *Il pensiero occidentale dalle origini ad oggi*, vol. 3, Brescia 1983, p. 449.

Reflections On
Theological Knowledge

from the Perspective of the Charism of Unity

Fr. Piero Coda, professor of fundamental theology at the Lateran University in Rome, introduces an original methodology of theology which derives from the method of the Abba School: "a dwelling in unity in Jesus" as the "way to knowing God in God." He goes on to describe unity and Jesus forsaken not so much as topics to be studied but rather as rich and promising forms of theological knowing.

In this article I will touch on three points suggested by its title.

First, I will try to explain the nature of Christian theology from the perspective of the experience of the Abba School. Since 1991 this school has tried to maintain a steady focus on the content and the method suggested by the charism of unity of the Focolare Movement and what it has brought to light.

In the second and third points, I will try to say something about the two principal "pillars," as Chiara Lubich calls them, of the theology that springs from this charism: unity and Jesus forsaken. I will treat them, however, not so much as theological topics but above all as constituting *ways* or *methods* of "doing theology."

The theology of Jesus

Theology, as we know, expresses itself in many forms. There is a critical-scientific theology, a more sapiential theology, and a mystical theology. Theology can have as many faces as practitioners. Augustine is not Aquinas; Maximus the Confessor is not Luther. Yet, there is something essential that defines Christian theology as theology. We can say that theology is knowing God in God through participation in the life of Jesus Christ.

Christian theology, then, is not simply a question of knowing God, as if God were an object outside of ourselves, but of knowing God in God, which expresses the participation, given us through Christ, in that knowledge that God has of himself and, in himself, of all that is. The term "knowing God in God" also underlines that theology is above all a way of "being," of "remaining" in God that, of course, blossoms into a corresponding knowledge.

It is no trivial observation when Chiara Lubich, in defining Christian existence in the light of the spiritual experience awakened by the charism of unity, says that we are already now "in the bosom of the Father," through the presence of the risen Jesus who makes us one in himself, and that we know in a new manner because of this unique "being-there."

The knowledge of God in God is, in fact, the ultimate goal towards which human knowledge tends. Aware of their incapacity to attain the goal by their own strength alone, people's search for knowledge is nonetheless sustained by the undying desire to find fulfillment beyond themselves, in fact, in God. All religious traditions and all the great seekers of God testify to this.

In one way or another, the human person realizes that he is willed, loved, made by Another. He thus knows that he is known, in the deepest fibers of his being and in the most profound meaning of his history, by Someone. For the same reason, he desires to know as he is known: to know him who knows me, and to know myself as I am known. Augustine writes in his *Confessions*: "I will know you, my knower, I will know you as I am known" (cf. 1 Cor 13:12).[1]

In that desire to know God that constitutes the human person there exists a hidden desire for reciprocity. Ultimately, he desires to love as he is loved.

In Jesus, this nostalgia and yearning become reality. In Matthew's Gospel (and in a parallel text in Luke; the entire Gospel of John seems to be built on this reality), Jesus says, "All things have been delivered to me by my Father. No one knows the Son except the Father, and no one knows the Father except the Son—and anyone to whom the Son chooses to reveal him" (Mt 11:27). Jesus knows the Father as he is known by him, and he wishes to communicate this knowledge to us.

Jesus can do this because he is the Son of God, God the Son—the Word—made man. As Son, he lives in full communion with his Father in every moment of his existence. This does not mean Jesus is dispensed from "growing" and from "learning" to know the Father and, in light of the Father, people, events, and the unfolding of the plan of salvation. Jesus is, after all, true God and true man. Luke writes that "Jesus increased in wisdom, and in stature and in favor" (2:52), and the letter to the Hebrews states that "although he was a son, he learned obedience through what he suffered" (5:8).

Jesus grows as man in his knowledge of the Father. Moreover, and paradoxically, he comes to know the Father in the form and measure that he is known by the Father only when he experiences his abandonment and death, when he entrusts himself to the One who knows him—at the very moment when Jesus himself no longer humanly knows Him.

The full blossoming of this knowledge is manifested in the Resurrection. Thanks to the Holy Spirit, the risen Lord is the event of perfect reciprocal immanence of the Father and of the Son, even in his humanity. This reciprocity finds expression in the "face to face" (cf. 1 Cor 13:12) knowledge that the Father has of the Son, and the Son, also as man, has of the Father.

Jesus, glorified by the Spirit, now appears to his disciples as the revelation of this reality, which is now extended to human beings through grace.

This is the core of what we can call the theology "of" Jesus: the knowledge of God lived by Jesus two thousand years ago, today, and forever, inasmuch as the risen Jesus has ascended with his humanity to the bosom of the Father and there embraces and contains in himself every time and place. This is the very knowledge of God that Jesus reveals and transmits to us in faith. Paul writes, "And because you are sons, God has sent the Spirit of his Son into our hearts crying 'Abba! Father!'" (Gal 4:6).

We are speaking of a knowledge that is simultaneously in the "already" and in the "not yet." It is in the "already" because human existence, through faith, baptism, and the eucharist, is truly grafted into the event of Christ crucified and risen, and therefore can share in his very knowledge of God in God. At the same time, it is in the "not yet" because human existence remains in time and therefore is subject to the dynamics of human growth and its limits; it awaits its completion from God, in Jesus who will come at the end of time.

In any case, if we take seriously the ontological novelty introduced into creation by the Incarnation, death, and Resurrection of the Son of God, and by the outpouring of the Holy Spirit, we cannot minimize the importance of this event for the knowledge (already now—in history) that we can have of God in Christ, thanks to the gift "without measure" of the Holy Spirit (cf. Jn 3:34).

We recall how Paul, in his first letter to the Corinthians, illustrates the novelty of this knowledge of God in the Spirit that Christ shares with us:

> "What no eye has seen, nor ear heard, nor the heart of man conceived, what God has prepared for those who love him," God has revealed to us through the Spirit. For the Spirit searches everything, even the depths of God.

For what person knows a man's thoughts except the spirit
of the man which is in him? So also no one comprehends
the thoughts of God except the Spirit of God. Now we
have received not the spirit of the world, but the Spirit
which is from God, that we might understand the gifts
bestowed on us by God . . . . "For who has known the
mind of the Lord so as to instruct him?" But we have the
mind of Christ. (1 Cor 2:9–12, 16)

"We have the mind of Christ."

The great tradition of Christian theology was born from and
has always been conscious of this extraordinary novelty.
Thomas Aquinas is a good example because the self-awareness
of the Catholic Church has seen in him the *Doctor communis,*
but we could cite innumerable other witnesses from the Christian East and West. Thomas writes: "Faith is assimilation to
the divine knowledge, since by means of the faith infused in us
we are united to the first truth through itself; and thus
immersed in the divine knowledge, we know all things so to
say with the eye of God."[2]

Therefore, when Thomas defines theology, he affirms that
"God is the subject of this science" because "all realities are
treated in sacred doctrine *sub ratione Dei* [which we can translate: "in the light that is God," "according to the viewpoint
that is God"] either because they are God himself, or because
they are ordered to God who is origin and end."[3] The object of
theology, in Jesus, is God in himself and God "all in all": all
things, that is, seen by God and in God.

It would be interesting to examine the history of theology to
see how, albeit with different words and accents, this profound
awareness has been expressed both in the East and in the
West, in Catholic and in Protestant theology. And it would be
interesting to trace the growth, the crisis (for example in
modernity), and the maturation of this history.

Suffice it to say that for all the great theologians of every
age, it is clear that we share in the knowledge that Jesus has of
the Father if we are in him: through living charity, faith,

baptism and the eucharist, and the gifts of the Spirit. Of significant and often essential importance are the great charisms given by the Holy Spirit that constitute the vital *humus* of theology and often shed new light on the Christian mystery. Bonaventure draws, also theologically, from the charism of Francis, just as Aquinas draws from that of Dominic.

In this perspective, the question arises: in what way does Chiara Lubich's charism of unity constitute the *humus* and the source of illumination for an original theology?

Before attempting even a brief answer, it would be well to take an equally brief look at the history of theology to place into context the unique contribution of the charism of unity. The Fathers of the Church, from Irenaeus to John Damascene—as well as the great Scholastics from Anselm to Duns Scotus—all subscribe, while using different words, to the definition of theology given by Thomas Aquinas. Modernity, by contrast, has changed the picture considerably. The division between reason and faith, on the one hand, and between so-called speculative theology and mystical theology, on the other, has lead—at least in the West—to a privileging, first, of a more rational-doctrinal theology, and then of a theology of a historical-critical or critical-scientific type.

To be sure, this development also expresses a positive exigency that accords with the dynamism of the Incarnation of the divine in the human realized in Jesus Christ, an Incarnation that progressively penetrates into man's consciousness. This positive exigency is that of historicity, of the value of the human subject and his relation with the other—all positive concerns despite the occasional drift into absolutization that can lead into blind alleys. The theology that grew out of the Protestant Reformation (I am thinking of the Christocentrism of Luther, but also of the great Idealists) is not foreign to this sensitivity, which ultimately, I repeat, has its source in the event of Christ.

Towards the end of the nineteenth century, there began to reawaken the need to return to the great theology of the tradition, hence, to an integral, living and knowing in God through

Jesus Christ and in the dynamism of the Holy Spirit that would simultaneously do justice to the positive concerns of modernity, in particular to the historical and social dimension of knowledge. Indeed the retrieval of the tradition needs to occur precisely from within the unprecedented "trial of the faith" (John Paul II) in which we find ourselves, a trial expressed in the feeling of the "death of God." It is an exciting and moving experience to read the prophets of this "new theology": Rosmini and Newman, Florenskij and Bulgakov, Barth and Bonhoeffer, Blondel and Rahner, de Lubac and von Balthasar, and others. Dialogue, especially in these last few decades, with the great non-Christian religious traditions, has also required the opening of new horizons.

It is against this epochal backdrop that, as often happens in the history of the Church, the charism of unity makes its novel contribution. To be sure, this novelty is not absolute. The charism of unity also makes explicit what is contained in the revelation that occurred eschatologically in Christ and is thenceforth transmitted by the Church.

Theology and unity

The event that springs from the charism of unity is the experience of our being one in Christ Jesus.[4] Chiara Lubich describes the event thus:

> We understood that in consuming ourselves into one and in placing unity at the basis of our life journey, we were Jesus who was walking. He who is the Way was making himself the way in us. We were no longer ourselves, but He in us.

Unity, brought about and shaped by the charism given by God, is the crucible in which we are forged into Jesus. We know well what that means on a spiritual and existential level. Let us consider the intellectual level of this reality: the aspect of theology.

What happens if I live the knowledge of God with unity in Christ at its basis? Knowing is permeated with love; indeed, it becomes one with love.

On the one hand, knowing becomes listening and acceptance: listening to God who comes to me through his Word, but also listening to my neighbor (in whom Christ is present and in whose heart and mind resounds, with a unique accent, the Word of God that he or she has received). In this way—through love—I "lose" my thought, I "put it aside," I silence it in order to welcome the thought of Jesus.

On the other hand, my own knowledge becomes entirely a gift and a communication of self to the other. In formulating and expressing my thought, which takes shape within me from Jesus alive in the unity that the Spirit shares with me, I act out of love in order to communicate Jesus in me to Jesus in my neighbor. This happens in reciprocity, when there is unity, for my neighbor does the same in my regard.

In other words, the event of unity lived also on the level of knowledge makes us, through the grace of God activated by reciprocal love, one with Christ present in each of us, one with Christ in the other, and one with Christ among us.

This is how our being becomes love, entirely centered—to use an image dear to the mystics—on that point where it receives itself as love from God and gives itself in return as love to him and to one's neighbors. This happens in Jesus, in whom we are "one" (cf. Gal 3:28), through the gift of the Holy Spirit.

And so we become *in deed* what we already are by grace in Christ: other Christs (though each is still himself) because we are "clothed" in him. Unity makes our being—as individuals and as a body—an event in Christ Jesus. This is how we are able to say, with Paul, "we have the mind of Jesus."

We can *conceive of* God in Jesus because in unity we are *conceived*, so to speak, born together with him and in him, from the Father in the Holy Spirit, as sons in the Son. The Father, in Jesus, can also say of us: "You are my Son, today I have begotten you" (Acts 13:33; Heb 1:5).

Obviously, this depends both on myself and on the others, on our doing truly and fully all our parts so that God—on the basis of the grace of our engrafting into Jesus through faith, the sacraments, and our reciprocal love—can give the grace of unity that makes us fully Jesus.

The Abba School—as an experience of unity also on the level of knowledge—thus presents theology with an opportunity to rediscover its "home." The theological tradition speaks of "theological sources" from which we can draw the truth of revelation. The event of unity, therefore, gives focus to and realizes the "theological source" par excellence: Jesus himself, living in our midst, leads us to the bosom of the Abba, where he "is." Jesus himself says it: "In that day," the day of the Easter event actualized in the day of the Church lived as unity, "you will know that I am in my Father and you in me, and I in you" (Jn 14:20).

Significantly, the originality of this theology tends to be expressed in terms of the *theology of Jesus*. Not, to be sure, of the historical Jesus, but of the risen Lord who lives today in the Christians who participate in this event in a vital way.

The reality, the gift of unity—the event of Jesus in us and among us here and now—allows, and indeed, urges, this definition of theology. There is nothing presumptuous or enthusiastic here. To speak of the "theology of Jesus" is not an integralist attempt to possess Jesus and so to reduce him to our measure. It is rather to underline that in unity we tend to the total emptying of ourselves—also on the intellectual plane—in order to welcome and to put into practice, as Paul says, "the mind of Christ."

Theology can thus rediscover in the event of unity its own identity and deepest vocation to be a theology "of" Jesus. Therein lie also the clarity and balance—if we authentically live unity—of a theology that springs from the center of revelation; that grafts itself onto, and achieves, the tradition centered on the spiritual and intellectual journey of individual persons; and that responds to the fundamental exigencies of modern times.

We cannot adequately develop all these affirmations here. The main point I wish to underline is that the event of unity indicates a specific theological methodology whose essence is a rediscovery of Jesus himself, of that "dwelling" through unity in him, that is the *meta-hodos*, the way to know God in God.

I will briefly touch upon a few aspects that stem from this.

First, lived unity brings into full relief and power the reality of being Church, that alone enables the realization of the theology of Jesus. Being Church does not mean—I speak as a Catholic—simply living the faith, familiarizing oneself with Scripture and Tradition, being faithful to the Magisterium, and doing justice to the charisms and the *sensus fidelium*. It also means welcoming—by being crucified with Christ and living reciprocal love—the grace of unity which is the living Church in act. Within this unity, all of the realities that we have listed find both their place and their authentic meaning as "bearers of the word of God" in their reciprocal relationship, indeed, in their *perichoresis*.

Second: by living unity, being in Jesus, and becoming "clothed" with him, my person is united within myself. This is true not only in the sense that I experience a vital connection between existence and knowledge, and therefore between spirituality and theology, but also in the sense that my knowledge becomes imbued with love and my love becomes contemplation. The depth of my being (my true self that is already "hid with Christ in God" (cf. Col 3:3), becomes more and more able to know lovingly and to love knowingly.

Third: when I live unity, when I "am" in Jesus, the knowledge of God does not draw me away from the world, but places me (through my relationship with my neighbor) at the heart of the world where the Word of God placed himself through his Incarnation and his abandonment on the cross. It is true that, in order to know God in Jesus, I transcend this world in him in order to "enter" the bosom of the Father, but I do not therefore abandon the world, but rather know the world in God and God in the world (in *perichoresis*).

A final aspect: the theology of Jesus is one and many, just as God is One and Triune, and Jesus himself is one and is many. As I stated at the beginning, it is true that there are as many theologies as there are theologians, but it is also true that Christian theology is one because Jesus is one. Unity brings home this reality with unique clarity. True theological pluralism does not clash with the identity of the one theology, but is the latter's necessary expression. In every theology that takes the "tuning note" of unity, we must hear—as Chiara Lubich puts it—a single word pronounced "in infinite tones." It is the one Christ who "clothes" himself differently with each one of us and who expresses, through us in Christ, the knowing of God both in its unity and in its multiplicity.

In unity and through unity, theology, lived in its Trinitarian reality, can rediscover the "forgotten transcendental": beauty (von Balthasar). Indeed, theology itself becomes an epiphany of beauty.

Theology and Jesus forsaken

Until now I have touched upon only the first "pillar" of the theology that springs from the charism of unity. But the discussion of unity naturally brings us to the second "pillar." The second, in fact, is the key to the first, without which the first can neither be understood nor lived: Jesus forsaken.

In the experience and theological perspective that springs from the charism of unity, abandonment is not one particular aspect of Jesus among others; it is the reality that expresses the deepest essence of the event of Jesus himself, and therefore, of the revelation of God and of creation that Jesus himself is.

Here, too, I would like to begin with an idea of Chiara Lubich that is like a lightning flash that illumines an unfamiliar and surprising panorama:

> Jesus is Jesus forsaken. This is because Jesus is Savior and Redeemer; and he redeems when he pours the divine onto humanity through the wound of his abandonment,

which is the pupil of the eye of God on the world: an infinite void through which God looks upon us: the window of God opened wide onto the world and the window of humanity through which it sees God.

The eye of God on the world is the heart of Christ, but the pupil is that wound. The eye is the heart, for though the eye is the organ for seeing (in the Trinity the eye of God is the Word), God who is love can see only with his heart. In him, love and light are one.

The image of the eye, as a symbol of being known by, and of knowing, God is typical of mystical traditions in every time and place, which go so far as to teach that the human person is "all eye" when enraptured into the true knowledge of God in God. "All eye" is a vivid expression used to describe, with maximum density, the idea of knowing the self and all things in God as one is known by him.

Thomas Aquinas himself, who is usually very prudent, affirms that faith, as we have said, is knowing "as it were with the eye of God." Catherine of Siena more boldly defines faith as "the pupil of the eye of the intelligence."[5]

Chiara Lubich's image goes further still. First, it confirms the reciprocity that is constitutive of knowing God: we know God because he first knows us. If the Word, in fact, is the eye with which God knows, then Jesus forsaken, the Word Incarnate in the fullness of the divine purpose, is "the pupil of the eye of God on the world."

God, therefore, knows the world—with a knowledge that is completely one with love—in Jesus forsaken. And only because God—in "the fullness of time" that touches and harbors within itself all time—knows us in Jesus forsaken, we in our turn and in response can know God as he knows us "in" Jesus forsaken.

But there is another aspect that Chiara Lubich underlines. It is clear that to know God in the manner of God, *to know in God*, we must transcend our simply human mode of knowing, we must let it go, abandon it. God—as God—is known only by God. The mystics and the great theologians say the same thing when they recover the centrality of "the theology of the cross" as the principal form of doing theology; or when they speak of an "apophatic" (negative) theology, which does not simply deny with one's own intelligence the still partial and provisional knowledge one has acquired of God, but denies the intelligence itself in order to know God, not "humanly" but "divinely"—with one's own intelligence, of course, but as "lost" and "found" again anew in Christ.

Bonaventure, for example, in the last part of his *Itinerarium mentis in Deum*, says that at the summit of the road to knowing God one must make an exodus from this world to the Father through Christ crucified. As is well known, he writes these pages at La Verna, contemplating the stigmata of Francis, his "being crucified with Christ."

Chiara Lubich sees the depth of the crucified in Jesus forsaken, who, as she herself explains, "loses God for God." He loses, that is—if we see everything from the viewpoint that interests us here—the knowledge that he has of the Father out of love for him and for us and, in so doing, makes himself "absolute emptiness" like the pupil of the eye of which Chiara Lubich speaks.

It is precisely thus that he comes to know the Father as he is known by him, even as a man, in the glorifying light of the Holy Spirit. It is in this way that Jesus forsaken is not only the "window of God opened wide upon the world," but also the "window of humanity through which it can see God."

Jesus forsaken, before being a topic of theology, is therefore theological knowledge itself in its root and its basic dynamism. When Paul in his first letter to the Corinthians says that he knows nothing "except Jesus Christ and him crucified" (1 Cor 2:2), he is also referring to this decisive and unique dimension of knowledge within faith.

The charism of unity centers our attention on Jesus forsaken. This is the novelty, the "something more" that informs the theology to which it gives birth. For the same reason, it underlines that the loss of the exercise of one's own intelligence that is needed in order to know God in the manner of God is not primarily an individual act of intellectual asceticism, but the act of love with which I make myself one with Jesus forsaken out of love for the Father and for my brothers "as" Christ loves them (cf. Jn 15:12–13). This "loss" is an act that is the way to the Resurrection of my intelligence, which rises imbued with the Holy Spirit in the risen Lord who lives in the bosom of the Father.

In reality, the becoming one of intelligence and love, which in speaking of unity we said constitutes and expresses the center of our being in the act of receiving ourselves and giving ourselves back to God, is Jesus forsaken; better yet, this unification occurs in Jesus forsaken when we make ourselves one with him because he made himself, and continues to make himself, one with us. Therefore we know and are born together, through Christ's "wound," as children of the Father who know the Father in the Spirit as we are known by him.

At this point, I would like to add a further important clarification. Jesus forsaken, as the full unfolding of Jesus, is the full revelation of the identity of God and of the identity of the human creature.

Chiara Lubich, in an oft-cited, richly pregnant text, puts it like this:

> Jesus forsaken, because he is not, is.
> We are if we are not.

Jesus forsaken—"the bowels of revelation," according to Antonio Rosmini—thus gives birth to an ontology, a decisively new vision of being. This new ontology is one of the more theologically original, even striking, consequences of this charism of unity. But it is a delicate consequence that needs to be understood and expressed in conformity with the vision of the charism. I will try to explain it properly as I have understood it and as Chiara Lubich has confirmed it.

First of all, the language of being/not being, which expresses the dynamic of love glimpsed in the light of Jesus forsaken, is fully legitimate for describing the being of the divine Persons within the Trinity.

In fact, as tradition explains (in particular Augustine and Aquinas), the divine Persons subsist only in relation, indeed *as* relation, which, being love, is a total and real giving of Oneself to the Other.

Contemplating Jesus forsaken, we can go further and say that in God each Person is *because he is not*. The Father, for example, is Father because he generates the Son, but in generating the Son, he gives his entire being, sharing with him his entire divine life. The Father's giving is real—so real that, to speak humanly, he strips himself completely of his being. And precisely in doing so, "he is," he *is* Father.

This absolute movement of being/not being is proper to God and to God alone. Created persons, by themselves, cannot accomplish this act, precisely because they are created; that is, they receive being from God and therefore cannot strip themselves of it *ontologically*. At most they can deny themselves, lose themselves intentionally (on the level of the actions of knowledge and love). But they cannot go so far as lose their being totally as being. Only in death can the created person let go—into the hands of God—of his entire being.[6]

Jesus forsaken, however, brings about a "new creation" in which the created person, destined by grace, can reach fulfillment. Jesus forsaken is the Word become man who lives his Trinitarian relationship of being/not being with the Father through the Holy Spirit in his humanity. The humanity of Jesus, because it is personally united to the Word, can in an abandonment and death accepted and lived out of love, experience the Son's dizzying self-effacement as love, thereby becoming fully introduced into the Trinitarian life.

The created person, then, can share in this reality only insofar as he is grafted onto Jesus forsaken—an engrafting that he must freely accept and live out through grace. It is not by chance that Paul speaks of "dying" and "rising" *with Christ* (cf. Rom 6:4–5). It is not simply an expression but a reality, even if our awareness normally touches only the smallest part of this event, and even if this reality, in all its ontological depth, will be fully disclosed only in its eschatological completion.

In short, we may legitimately use the language of being/not being to express love (being as love) not only in reference to the triune God but, through Jesus forsaken, also in reference to human persons. We begin to see, then, the sort of ontology radically rethought in Christ that Klaus Hemmerle glimpsed and had begun to sketch before his death.[7]

Conclusion

A word to conclude.

Speaking of theology in the light of the charism of unity, we have touched on two points: unity and Jesus forsaken. We have seen how—conceived more as forms of theological knowing than as topics—these two points seem to bring the deepest vocation of theology to an unexpected completion. Since this is so, we might then ask: is it even possible today to do theology without unity and Jesus forsaken? The horizons that this way of doing theology is opening for ecumenical and interreligious dialogue and for modern thought are beginning to show that the answer must be a resounding no.

To use an image from Chiara Lubich, a theology that begins with unity and Jesus forsaken is like the flowering of a tree that has been growing throughout the centuries precisely for that purpose. It seems particularly clear that this blossoming will also require a refashioning of theological knowledge in its concrete expression. The history of theology has known many models, many systematic forms: from the biblical commentaries of the Fathers, to the medieval *Summae,* to the tractates of the manualists.

Can we offer an hypothesis about the form a theology would take if it is inspired and nourished by the charism of unity? Without claiming, obviously, to offer a definitive answer, I would hazard two words: journeying and *perichoresis*.

Journeying. If theology is the knowing in God that we have described, it is by its very nature an event. If it is a theology of Jesus, which occurs in him, and in him forsaken, as the way to the Father, theology becomes a *"viam agere,"* a "being under way," a journey: it becomes "acting in truth" of which the Fourth Gospel speaks (cf. Jn 3:31). Exegesis and systematics, dogmatics and moral theology, mysticism and critical scholarship, remain distinct and necessary on their own respective planes, but they all can find a new dynamic unity in this "journeying."

Perichoresis. If one is in Jesus, and in Jesus in the bosom of the Father, one can know things as God knows them. God knows them in himself, in the One who is Triune, and he knows them at the same time in the Word Incarnate, crucified and risen, in whom God and man are united and distinct, "without confusion and without separation." God knows them, from the point of view of eschatology, when he is "all in all" (cf. 1 Cor 15:28), for then each thing will be all others (in God). Chiara Lubich captures the sense of participation in this divine-human knowledge in the risen Lord with a new and vivid neologism: "trinitization." This term means that what we have called "theology of Jesus" "already" has this form, though "not yet" in its fullness. In this theology, therefore, each reality can be known only as having in itself all the others, in a Trinitarian relation with these others in the light of Jesus forsaken and of unity.

> In the mystery of God we find a similarity to the fraction of the Host: in each piece there is the entire Jesus. If you break apart the great mystery of Christian life, each piece holds the entire mystery. Why is this? Because all of us and creation itself are destined to become God. Therefore each holds in itself all. This is a new theological vision.

We glimpse the revolution in methodology this brings. We can do so because in every act of true love, in every lived encounter with Jesus forsaken, we find everything, everything that remains because it is, because it is God (in us).

Piero Coda

Notes

1. *Confessions* 10, 1, 1.
2. *In Boethium de Trinitate*, q. III, a. 1.
3. *Summa Theologiae*, q. I, a. 7.
4. Cf. "Sulla teologia che scaturisce dal carisma dell'unità," in *Nuova Umanità* XVIII (1996), 104: 155–166.
5. Catherine of Siena, *Dialogue* 45.
6. Von Balthasar explains: "Absolute self-giving of this kind cannot exist in the creaturely realm, since man has no control over his existence and, hence, over his 'I', and 'we cannot give away that over which we have no control.' We must try to grasp the fact that where absolute Being is concerned, Being that has possession of itself, 'divine self-possession expresses itself in perfect self-giving and reciprocal surrender; furthermore the creature's own existence, over which it has no control, is drawn into this movement. . . .' In giving himself, the Father does not give something (or even everything) that he *has* but all that he *is* . . . so the Father's being passes over, without remainder, to the begotten Son. . . . This total self-giving, to which the Son and the Spirit respond by an equal self-giving, is a kind of 'death,' a first, radical 'kenosis'; as one might say, it is a kind of 'super-death.' " H. U. von Balthasar, *Theodrama. Theological Dramatic Theory V: The Last Act*, San Francisco 1998, pp. 82–84.
7. Klaus Hemmerle, *Thesen zu einer trinitarischen Ontologie*, Freiburg 1992.

(First published in *Communio* 28 [Fall 2001]. Reprinted with permission.)

The Charism of Unity

in the Light of the Mystical Experience
of Chiara Lubich

Biblical scholar Gerard Rosse, attempting an interpretation of the mystical experience lived by Chiara Lubich in the summer of 1949, treats its important theme of unity.

I would like to attempt an interpretation of the mystical experience lived by Chiara Lubich in the summer of 1949.

For readers who may not know its context I must give some background. Already back in World War II, Chiara Lubich, along with other young women, had the experience of evangelizing her life by living the Word together in a group; they were therefore trained in the life of communion.

In July of 1949 this same group of women and some of the first men Focolarini went to the Dolomite Mountains for vacation. They were joined by Igino Giordani, a highly renowned Catholic politician, journalist, and scholar, a man they fondly called Foco (meaning fire). Chiara gave a name to this group that shared her mystical experience of 1949; she called it *Anima*, the "Soul."

This is how she recalls her experience:

> Foco, enchanted with Catherine of Siena, had throughout his life sought a virgin to follow. Feeling he discovered her among our little group, he approached me

one day proposing to make a vow of obedience to me. By doing so, he thought he would be obeying God. In that moment I neither understood the reason for obedience nor for this type of unity among two people. At the same time, however, it seemed to me that Foco was under a grace that shouldn't be lost.

So I said to him, "It could really be that what you feel comes from God. Tomorrow in church, then, when I receive Jesus in the eucharist in my heart, as in an empty chalice, I will tell him: 'on my nothingness, make a pact of unity with Jesus in the eucharist in Foco's heart. And bring about that bond between us as you see it should be.'" I then added, "And Foco, you do the same."

The following day, after having made this pact, we left the church. Foco had to conduct a conference for the friars there. I felt urged to go back into church. I entered and went before the tabernacle. Wanting to pray to Jesus in the eucharist, I was about to call his name, Jesus. But I couldn't. That Jesus who was in the tabernacle was also in me. I was still myself, but made another him. I could not therefore call myself. In that moment a word spontaneously came from my mouth, "Father," and I found myself in the bosom of the Father.

So began Chiara's mystical experience. I'll now turn to the words of the pact, which contain the characteristic elements of the charism of unity.

The eucharist is clearly its foundation. Two characteristics of this sacrament come to light in the pact.

1. The eucharist existed beforehand, and it comes from God through the mediation of the Church. The eucharist tells us therefore of the divine origin of what is about to happen; it is not due to Chiara's initiative. Her human contribution is her total openness that enables Jesus in the eucharist to express the best of his potential. Furthermore, if the reality called Soul is born on the basis of the eucharist, it is born within the Church and consequently can never pose itself in competition with the Church or become a church within the Church, but

only be a reality that *is* Church at the service of the one Church of God.

2. The other characteristic of the eucharist that comes to light in the pact is its ecclesial-communitarian dimension. It is not only bread of life for the individual but sacrament of unity, of Christ's body. We recall the First Letter to the Corinthians: "Because the loaf of bread is one, we, many though we are, are one body, for we all partake of the one loaf" (10:17).

Another fundamental element of the pact that is intimately linked with the eucharist is *mutual love*. The bond between the eucharist and mutual love is clearly a constant theme in the teaching of the New Testament and in the Tradition of the Church.

Since the eucharist is in its vital reality a sacrament of unity, love lived reciprocally renders it effective in everyday life. By living in unity, believers are inseparably both Church and Christ (while also keeping their distinction).

An original aspect of this charism emerges: the reality called Soul brings about something that constitutes the Church.

More precisely, the text of the pact does not explicitly speak of reciprocal love, but rather of nothingness. This nothingness, however, is not something added on to love as though it were a third element, but expresses instead the quality of that love. Furthermore, this nothingness is not lived as a private relationship with Jesus in the eucharist but in reciprocity with others. Finally, this nothingness has a specific face: Jesus forsaken, who constitutes the quality and the measure of that nothingness. In the same text of 1949, we also read:

> We must be the nothingness of Jesus forsaken, who is infinite nothingness. The Holy Spirit will then dwell within us.

Nothingness refers therefore to Jesus forsaken, not to a humility lived to an extreme degree or to an ascetical ideal. Nothingness brings together three realities of the life of faith:

1. The baptismal reality of having died with Christ as a participation in the vivifying death of Christ; it is a gift of God and expresses the sacramental effectiveness of agape.

2. The life of agape in its dynamic of non-being/being, which actualizes our baptism.

3. Jesus forsaken, who constitutes the eschatological reality of agape (the nothingness that brings forth the Holy Spirit), and its measure in the perennial disposition of losing God for God in human relationships.

In this space, born from a reciprocal nothingness with the readiness to lose God for God, the eucharist as an effective sign has actualized its potential as sacrament of the body of Christ; the "all are one in Christ Jesus" (Gal 3:28) is realized in its Christological dimension (the presence of Christ in the midst that unites and distinguishes) and in its ecclesial dimension (the community as the body of Christ).

In the reciprocal nothingness of the pact, we find what constitutes the originality of the charism of unity. In this nothingness of reciprocal love the Spirit of Christ can manifest himself in the greatest degree of purity and fullness our human limits allow, since we are then less affected or colored by our personal attachments, points of view, and subjectivism. The risen Lord can best express himself.

Thus Chiara can write:

> It is no longer we who live
> but Christ who truly lives in us,

so giving the word of Paul (Gal 2:20) not only its full personal dimension but an ecclesial one as well, a personal dimension enriched by that of the Church.

The originality comes through in the word *truly*, which expresses both the novelty and the continuity of the Soul in the Church. Of course, the Church was always the body of Christ, but now there is something more. This "more" does not consist in the revelation of a new set of truths, nor is it measured in quantifying terms, but is a life that can renew what already exists. A new life springs forth from the womb of the Church itself, not from outside of it; a divine injection that has become an event in history. The Church, looking upon this new creature, the Soul, has seen with surprise its very own mystery reflected in the Soul in a clearer way than ever before.

Chiara defines the Soul thus:

> The Soul is the Church, in the sense that for Church we mean Unity, that is, the fullness of Christian life.

The Growth of the Soul

Through Chiara's mystical journey, the Soul, as a living creature that grows and develops, acquires the features of the Church.

As we have seen in the pact, the Soul was born with the face of Christ-Church. But the Soul, since it is Church, is also distinct from Christ and finds the fullness of its relationship with Christ with whom it was first identified: the Soul acquires the face of Bride. Therefore, from its unity-identity, that is, from its experience of Church as the body of Christ, the Soul passes on to unity-distinction, the experience of being Bride of Christ.

> Only now, after our souls have, through Jesus among them, espoused one another and are Church, can they say—whether in unity with others or individually (each has the value of the whole, of Jesus among them)—they are spouses of Christ.

Therefore, in the unity lived in that reciprocal nothingness, each one participates in the fullness of relationship with Christ that only the Church possesses: that of being Bride.

To be Bride, one must be a complete person, that is, possess a personality capable of loving. Yves Congar explains: "The unity of the Person-Church as Bride radically supposes the unity of humanity as a complete entity able to receive grace. This comes about as an imitation and extension of the original disposition of Mary lived by a multitude of persons, who participate in Christ by way of grace and thus form his body."[1] In other words, and applied to this case, Jesus, giving to the Soul a personality to be able to make her his Bride, communicates to her his own Self. Chiara expresses it in the following sentence:

> Jesus cannot espouse but Jesus, since he cannot be one but with himself.

The characteristic of the espousal love of the Bride lies in her total openness to the love of her Spouse. (We recall the ecclesiology that forms the background of Ephesians 5:21.) And here the Church-Bride, whose Self is Christ present, assumes the face of Mary; she acquires the Marian profile. The Soul has the experience of being Mary, an experience Chiara lives mystically and recounts in this way:

> One day one of us had proposed that we consecrate ourselves to Mary, meaning to consecrate the Soul to Mary. All agreed, and at Holy Communion in the morning each asked Jesus in the eucharist to consecrate, as he saw fit, the Soul to Mary, and that he then tell us what had taken place in us. As soon as we asked for this, the Soul understood that it had become Mary, the Soul understood immediately that Jesus, in consecrating us *to* Mary, was consecrating *us* Mary, making us sacred with Mary as Mary.

Being Mary expresses another face of the Soul made Church. Mary-Church is humanity made One, created by Christ, and humanity responding personally to the love of Christ, who has given it life by saving it. Again we find a reference to Ephesians (5:21ff) that is revealing: Christ gave himself for the Church to make it holy, "to present to himself a glorious church, holy and immaculate" (Eph 5:27). Chiara is not referring here to the baptismal immaculatization, but the full actualization of the baptismal reality that is produced by the eucharist in a life of unity.

But the Soul-Mary, Bride of Christ, is not yet the arrival point. In fact, in her union with her Spouse, the Church becomes Mother: in the life of unity, the Soul generates Christ in the world. We find in Chiara's account a description of this new phase of the mystical journey she lived in 1949:

> But what happened afterward was more marvelous still. On the following day we went to Holy Communion. As soon as I received Jesus, I distinctly heard, with the ears of my soul, a voice: in your flesh I now form my own Son or, better, I transform your flesh into the flesh of Jesus, making you another Jesus in the truest sense of the word.

Again upon receiving the eucharist, the sacrament par excellence of the Church as Unity, another mystical experience occurred: the Soul, being Mary, becomes another Jesus. Now, through this spousal union, the Soul-Mary-Church not only becomes the tabernacle of Jesus present in her midst (as already experienced in the pact), but also Mother in being able to give this Christ to the world, generating him outside of herself. In this way the Soul has reached a new maturity: being Mary, she has become capable of offering the world the *true* face of Christ, the one generated in the life of unity. And so the Soul has been prepared for her work in the Church, which Chiara describes:

> Our Ideal—we see it always more clearly—is no other than a divine injection so that the mystical body, the Church, might live its divine life in fullness. This is why the Focolare was born, so that in the unity of two or more they might offer Jesus to the faithful to make of them other Jesuses, living and healthy members of the mystical body.

Through these steps, the Soul has matured and been placed on its mission: that of bringing to light, outside of herself, that Jesus generated in those within herself.

In the reciprocal nothingness of the pact, we find all that constitutes the originality, that "something more" as it were, that the charism of unity has to offer the Church and the world: the face of the risen Christ among us. In the nothingness of reciprocal love, the Spirit of Christ can manifest himself better for the needs of the present-day Church. The charism of unity has given light to a spirituality that typifies the ecclesiology of communion regiven its honor by the Second Vatican Council.

The Charism of Unity
in the Ecclesiology of Communion

Now I would like to highlight some of the ecclesial characteristics that emerge from the spirituality born from this charism: a *spirituality of communion*; an *ethics that is typically Christian*; a *way of sanctity* that is authentically ecclesial.

The Spirituality of communion

By the nature of the pact itself, the fullness of Jesus emerges in reciprocal nothingness: the mediation of our neighbor is indispensable.

We know that baptism incorporates the believer into Christ at the same time in which it introduces him or her into the community. The horizontal and vertical relationships are inseparably linked and relative one to the other: personal relationship with God is always lived and developed in fraternal communion.

The ecclesial dimension has therefore been present in the Christian life of all times. But was its novelty really understood? Did it always hold its rightful place? We cannot deny that the dominant spirituality in the Church of the last centuries has had a prevailing individual stamp.

Biblical and patristic studies, already before the Second World War, have brought a dimension of communion back to its rightful place in Christian life. (I recall the so-called *Nouvelle Theologie* in France and the studies of Mersch and of Cerfaux on the Church as the body of Christ.) These were still on the intellectual level, however, though attempts were certainly made to translate these studies into life. But a light from God was needed to give the key to its application, a "cell" that shares the very same substance of the Church, that could incarnate the reality of Unity and give witness to it. I think that God has given us the charism of unity as one of the necessary contributions to our times.

The spirituality of communion reveals itself to be the spirituality most in conformity with the reality of the Church, the body of Christ; it is born from the very nature of the Church.

Its logic is found in the dual commandment of love of God and love of neighbor: the believer loves God by doing his will, which is love of neighbor. The agape that comes from God always wants to be directed to our neighbors: this way we live within our communion with God (cf. Jn 15:9). This same logic appears, for example, in the parable of the ruthless servant (Mt 18:23). The concrete response that the king expects from his servant whose enormous debt he forgave was that the servant do likewise for his debtors; only in this way can he remain in the friendship of his king.

Our neighbor takes on the importance, then, of being a mediator of God.

> I understood that I was created as a gift for the one next to me, and the one next to me was created as a gift for me. As the Father in the Trinity is everything for the Son and the Son everything for the Father.

In the gift of one to the other, each becomes for the other a source of the fullness of divine life. We can say that our neighbor becomes the eucharist of every moment, as a text of Chiara's suggests:

> As one Host of the millions of Hosts on earth is enough to nourish oneself of God, one neighbor is enough (the one that the will of God places next to us) to be in communion with the mystical Jesus.

In the spirituality of communion, our neighbor is re-established in his or her true place: not as a distraction to our recollection nor an obstacle in our personal union with God, but as the privileged moment of communion lived with him. Thanks to my neighbor I am Church, I am enriched by the presence in me of Christ present in the midst of human relationships.

The spirituality of communion born from this charism without doubt responds to the needs of the authentic ecclesiology of communion proposed by the Second Vatican Council (*Lumen gentium, Gaudium et spes*). The new awareness of the mystery of the Church as the sacrament of Christ, where the variety itself of gifts is a witness of the unity of the body of Christ, where "there remains, nevertheless, a true equality between all with regard to the dignity and to the activity which is common to all the faithful in the building up of the body of Christ" (LG 32), and where "all in the Church are called to holiness" (LG 39), has surpassed the concept of Church as an "unequal society" (present in papal documents all the way up to Pius X).

Pope John Paul II, in his *Novo millennio ineunte,* released in the year 2000, repeatedly underlines that such a spirituality of communion must characterize Christian commitment in the third millennium. "To make the Church the home and the school of communion: that is the great challenge facing us in the millennium which is now beginning, if we wish to be faithful to God's plan and respond to the world's deepest yearnings" (43).

He underlines therefore the need to "promote a spirituality of communion" that can animate and penetrate all the sectors of ecclesial and human life. "Spirituality of communion" is first of all the awareness that, together with others, one is a member of the one body of Christ, brought into the intimate life of God.

As a consequence, the Pope asks for attention to one's neighbors, to be one with them in their joys and sorrows, to see what is positive in others, to make room for them in our own hearts. These are concrete actions to take.

Naturally, it is love that surfaces as the life of a spirituality of communion. In fact, "communion is the fruit and demonstration of that love which springs from the heart of the Eternal Father and is poured out upon us through the Spirit which Jesus gives us (cf. Rom 5:5), to make us all 'one heart and one soul' (Acts 4:32)" (42). The popes, as does the Second Vatican Council, will stress the preferential option for the poor, according to the spirit of the gospel.

But now let's look at the characteristics of Christian ethics in the perspective of an ecclesiology of communion, as it appears in the charism of Chiara.

Christian ethics

Christian ethics is anchored in faith. It is the consequence of what Christians already have received and must allow to develop in themselves: the divine life. Christian ethics will tend, therefore, not to build up a good Christian but to shape a behavior that is conforming to the *new creation*. Authentic Christian morals tend to create in the life of the believer what he or she has already become by grace.

In other words, Christian ethics is above all *paschal ethics;* it is the consequential result of dying and rising in Christ (A. Schweitzer) or, as F. X. Durrwell writes, "The Holy Spirit who raises Christ is the law of the New Testament."[2] And in the words of Paul: "Since we live by the spirit, let us follow the spirit's lead" (Gal 5:25). Christian ethics is therefore a dying to oneself (nothingness), a dying that leaves room for the activity of the Spirit of Christ. It is in this perspective that the following text of Chiara's should be understood:

> Love must be distilled to the point of being the Holy Spirit. It is distilled by passing through Jesus forsaken. Jesus forsaken is the nothingness.

Love as agape must pass through the purification of death. But this purification does not come from long penances but from a faith that expresses itself through love (Gal 5:6) and, more precisely, through mutual love, in reciprocity, and therefore in the ecclesial dimension of Christian life. In the non-being that characterizes the dynamics of agape, purification is the work of God.

Consequently, in authentic Christian morals the logic is reversed. It is not a question of living well in order to perfect one's own self; it is a question of losing this self to receive it back new from God. God is not satisfied with forming a virtuous person; he wants a new creation, which only the nothingness of reciprocal love can create.

We find this new logic in the following text:

> Who lives in one's neighbor does not possess the virtues as usually intended: one is nothingness, and nothingness has nothingness: it does not have purity, nor humility, nor patience, nor mortification, etc., because one is nothingness; therefore the true purity is purity of purity, true humility is humility of humility, true patience is patience of patience, etc.

Love in this text appears truly to be the queen of Christian life; it does not shun anything, but brings everything to its eschatological destination. The virtues appear as the thousands of faces of the nothingness of love. In other words, love in the paschal nothingness lived by the believer displays itself in many colors, not as works of one's own self but as gifts of the Spirit.

Christian ethics is paschal ethics, but also ethics of a unity-communion. The qualities, talents and virtues of the individual do not serve primarily to form virtuous and balanced people but to favor a relationship with others. It is the Pauline ethics, in which all actions of the Christian, because he or she is a member of the body of Christ, serve its edification (Rom 14:19; 15:2; 1 Cor 8:1, etc.). It is a matter of concretizing, in a life of communion, the realities of the Church as Unity.

In the reciprocal nothingness of the pact, we find the central points of a Christian ethics that is truly ecclesial.

Christian holiness

In the logic of faith, God has given to the believer new life and therefore communion with God, the purpose of holiness. Consequently, the believer is called to become holy in order to grow in the holiness already received from God in Christ. In the following beautiful text, Paul confides: "I continue my pursuit in hope that I may possess it, since I have indeed been taken possession of by Christ [Jesus]" (Phil 3:12).

At Damascus, Paul was taken possession of by the risen Christ. This event gave his life new direction: to take possession of Christ. Paul uses a sports image to speak about holiness: "Brothers, I do not think of myself as having reached the finish line. I give no thought to what lies behind but push on to what is ahead. My entire attention is on the finish line as I run toward the prize to which God calls me—life on high in Christ Jesus" (Phil 3:13-14). It is not a matter of a breathless effort to reach a goal which is outside of him. For Paul, it is a matter of coming closer to Christ, who has already taken possession of him, and to grow toward Jesus, who lives in the depths of the believer.

How do we reach the Christ who lives in the most intimate center of our being?

Pseudo-Dionysius the Areopagite theorizes about a way that has become a classic in mysticism: an interior journey toward the center of the soul where the Holy Trinity lives. To take this road to union with God, silence is necessary as a distancing not only from the violence of the passions but also from material preoccupations, from the agitation of the world, from all that provokes dispersion. It is a long hard road, a slow process of purification and transformation, possible only to those living in suitable environments like monasteries. Furthermore, such a mystical way remains distant from a spirituality lived together with others in everyday life. The mystic certainly does not distance himself from the Church; quite the opposite. Passion for the Church is the fruit of a union with God that comes at the end of a long journey. From the solitude of the encounter with God, the mystic descends among others in the midst of the world, not ceasing, however, to remain isolated with God.

Therese of Lisieux discovered an accelerated way to union with God. She renounces building up her own self and instead entrusts herself totally and confidently to the hands of Jesus. He will be the one to bring her ahead. Here again, we find the logic of faith. But the little way for reaching union with the Spouse and for arriving at the heart of the Church is still an individual way and not lacking in its aridities.

The mystical life that is found in the writings of Chiara Lubich is more radical: in reciprocal nothingness, union with God, with Christ in the midst of believers, is full, immediate and open to everyone in *daily life*. We find ourselves in John's logic: "No one has ever seen God. Yet if we love one another God dwells in us, and his love is brought to perfection in us" (1 Jn 4:12). It is the mystical life of the Christian community as such.

Chiara likes to use the image of the mountain, not only because it is natural to her native surroundings (Trent), but even more because it refers to the experience of classical mysticism, the climb to the peak with which one often confronts oneself. But holiness need not be a distant goal that one climbs to, on a long ascetical journey. Chiara writes:

> Who enters the way of unity enters directly in the unitive way. Who enters the way of unity does not climb a mountain in fatigue but, through an initial and total thrust that implies the total death of self, one places oneself on the peak of the mountain.

We are back in the logic of faith. Holiness is the gift of God given at the beginning of the life of the baptized person and is to be lived in the present. The Christian vocation is not to reach a far away goal but to live in newness of life (Rom 6:4). The believer must make room for the Spirit present within. The solution proposed is a simple one: the reciprocal nothingness of love.

> We place this at our starting point: to love God with all our heart, soul, and strength, and therefore to love our neighbor as ourselves. Thus we begin our sanctification by sanctifying ourselves with others, in communion with our neighbors, and we do not even imagine the prospect of sanctifying ourselves individually.

In fact,

> by themselves, souls in good faith try to reach God without their neighbor and find the way arduous. After much time they reach the peak of the mountain where they ought to have started out.

The peak of the mountain is not the point of destination, but the point of departure. There is still a road to travel and trials do exist, but it is a matter of walking "along the mountain ridge all the way to God."

It is a growing in the holiness already received, a growing that manifests always more what we are already at the beginning:

A tree is not more perfect than the seed (the seed contains the tree), but what the seed contains is manifested more in the tree.

In John's mysticism, the journey is made by remaining in Christ (cf. Jn 15). This way of sanctity, consistent with the spirituality of unity, is also the typical way of the Church.

I attempted to bring to light the originality of the charism of unity; its incarnation in that little mystical body called the Soul; its specific place in the heart of the Church. Certainly, the gifts of God in the Church are numerous, and the charism of unity must be considered as a gift alongside the others at the service of the one body of Christ, at the service of humanity. Furthermore, if in a spirituality of communion the neighbor is a mediator of God, then so are the other charisms for the charism of unity.

Gerard Rosse

Notes

1. *La Personne "Eglise"* in *Revue Thomiste* 4, 1971, p. 629.
2. F. X. Durrwell, *La Risurrezione di Gesù,* Rome 1993, p. 188.

Forever Toward Disunity

Reflections on hell
in the thought of Chiara Lubich

Fr. Humbertus Blaumeiser, professor at the Gregorian University in Rome and expert in the theology of Martin Luther, gives a glimpse of what could be called the reverse side of the "coin" of unity, some strikingly acute ideas on the reality of "hell."

Speaking of hell today

While faith in the beyond is as old as humanity itself, hell is not a popular topic today. Some traditional notions of hell, such as a definite place, flames of fire, or torments, appear somewhat incredible. The rich creativity of writers and painters throughout the ages and the strong influence of ancient pagan literature have contributed to the image of hell as being something mythological, an image that makes it difficult to speak about it today. Jean-Paul Sartre in fact wrote: "So this is hell. No one would believe it. . . . Remember the sulfur, the wooden pyre, the grill. . . . What a joke! We don't need any grills; hell is other people."[1]

Yet Jesus definitely spoke about hell. Just think of the account of the final judgment in the Gospel of Matthew. "When the Son of Man comes in glory . . . all the nations will be assembled before him. And he will separate them one from another. . . . And these will go off to eternal punishment, but the righteous to eternal life" (Mt 25:31-32; 46). Luke's gospel recounts the parable of the rich glutton and the poor man named Lazarus: "Between us and you a great chasm is established to prevent anyone from crossing who might wish to go from our side to yours or from your side to ours" (Lk 16:26). Both accounts present us with a "beyond" which is clearly divided into two spheres. Our life can be fulfilled in communion with God eternally, or it can be forever doomed.

Referring to the second hypothesis, Jesus frequently used images taken from the Old Testament. They were well known among the Jews. He spoke of the eternal fire and the worm that never dies (see Is 66:24). In other places he made reference to darkness, and the wailing and grinding of teeth. Apart from these expressions, however, the New Testament gives us little information on what hell is really like. In this aspect it differs not only from the literature of later centuries but also from the apocrypha (the writings which are not among the accepted books of the Scripture). The New Testament does not intend to satisfy our curiosity about life after death; rather it aims at the here and now: the heights and depths of human freedom.[2] "Enter through the narrow gate," Jesus said, "for the gate is wide and the road broad that leads to destruction" (Mt 7:13).

At the heart of what is revealed to us about hell, therefore, is the possibility of eternal damnation. This, however, is what the modern mind finds hard to accept. Is it possible that God, being God, needs to punish evildoers and reward only the good? If God is love, how can he permit someone to be lost forever? "Would it not have been better," asked Jean Guitton, interpreting modern thinking, "not to have created at all rather than to have created a humanity which, as beautiful as it is, carries this eternal stain?"[3] There is always the hidden suspicion that hell is nothing more than the product of the sadistic imagination of those who advocate it, that it is the idea of people who obviously think they are exempt from such punishment, while holding that others are headed for it.

Scripture clearly states that God does not wish that "any should perish but that all should come to repentance" (2 Pt

3:9). Moreover, God "wills everyone to be saved" (1 Tm 2:4). With these words and other phrases in mind,[4] Hans Urs von Balthasar daringly expressed the hope that in reality no one would be lost forever: hell is a *real possibility*, but it has never been said that this possibility would come to pass.[5] It is not by chance that while "the Church has canonized many individuals, she has never pronounced anyone as damned, not even Judas."[6]

Some Fathers of the Church thought differently. Augustine in particular feared that most people would be lost to eternal damnation. The great medieval mystic, Saint Gertrude, had a different understanding. It is said that the Lord addressed these mysterious words to her: "I will not tell you what I have done with Solomon or Judas so that my mercy will not be abused."[7]

It is hard for us to imagine today the significant role that the fear of hell played in people's lives in the past. While the fear of hell may have produced anguish, it did encourage good moral behavior and social order. Themes on the "Last Things," such as death, judgment, heaven, hell and purgatory, easily found their place in sermons. John Paul II observed: "It could be said that these sermons, which correspond perfectly to the content of revelation in the Old and New Testaments, went to the very heart of man's inner world. They stirred his conscience, they threw him to his knees, they led him to the screen of the confessional, they had a profound salvific effect all their own."[8]

This type of fear now seems to have almost disappeared. A recent survey showed that those who do believe in a world beyond tend to imagine it in a positive light.[9] Some people, however, remarked that when the existence of hell was generally negated, hell itself spilled over onto the earth, and they cite the dramas of Auschwitz, Hiroshima and the Stalinist gulag.[10]

On the above premises, let us now enter our topic more directly. What new perspective can a theology centered on unity and Jesus forsaken uncover on the topic of hell?

Does God punish?

Where does the notion of hell come from? There are two likely answers.

The first is the most common and the simplest. At the end of time, God will reward good and punish evil. This is founded upon a basic concept of justice found in many cultures and religions. Its roots are found in the experience of human justice. With a biblical backing that speaks of final judgment and in keeping with the juridical mentality of the Romans and the Germans, this idea has played an important role in theology for centuries.

Nowadays, we better understand the limits of such a concept. How can we imagine a God who is love and mercy merely settling accounts with humankind at the end of the world? Doesn't this idea rather resemble human behavior? Thus comes to the fore another understanding of things: seeing hell as an *intrinsic* consequence of a person's actions rather than as a punishment.

This idea is found outside of Christianity as well. In Buddhist scriptures we find: "No one created hell. The burning spirit that gives in to anger produces the fire of hell which consumes whoever comes near. When a person does evil, he lights the fire of hell and is burned by his own fire."[11]

This may appear to be a purely psychological interpretation, but the following text by Paul Claudel clearly gives evidence to the Christian and transcendent dimension. "Whoever does not die in Christ and in communion with Christ, dies in his own likeness. He cannot change the imprint of himself, which in each moment of his life he has impressed upon the eternal substance." Claudel goes on to compare our life with the drafting of a text. "Until the final word is written," he writes, "the hand can go back and cross it off. But when it is finished it is as indestructible as the material upon which it is written."[12]

At the origin of eternal damnation, therefore, we find the human person, not God. "God creates heaven," Michel

Carrouges affirms, "but the rebellious creature creates hell. God creates freedom, but the creature can freely use it to create hell."[13] Among the great witnesses acknowledging this drama is Dostoyevski who, according to Carrouges, masterfully describes "the secret expansion of hell in the heart of human life, even before the flash of *judgment* reveals in a blazing light the tragic dualism of the world."[14]

We find a very balanced view about this in the *Catechism of the Catholic Church*. Referring to the universal judgment it states: "In the presence of Christ, who is Truth itself, the truth of each man's relationship with God will be laid bare. The Last Judgment will reveal even to its furthest consequences the good each person has done or failed to do during his earthly life" (n.1039).

In light of this, the idea of judgment and retribution is not abolished; rather it is seen and understood in a more ontological sense. The *Catechism* speaks of hell as the "state of definitive self-exclusion from communion with God and the blessed" (n.1033) and adds that God "predestines no one to go to hell" (n.1037; see n.1058).

Speaking about the next life, Chiara Lubich follows the same line of thought and frequently expresses her thinking with a very succinct image. She says that we build on earth the house we will inhabit in the next life. Some of her notes express this in more depth. But to understand them we need to first consider a wider perspective.

In Chiara Lubich's anthropological view, each one of us is a word of God pronounced by the Father in the Word which is the Son. This is our true self. Our entire life consists in fulfilling this profound reality about ourselves. Each person is called to become more and more that particular word in the Word, that "Idea" that the Father had when he called us into being. This is the only way that we can reach our true fulfillment and come to occupy the "place" which has been in the mind of God for us from all eternity.

Against this background we can read and understand the following text: "The scene of this world is fast escaping," Chiara writes, echoing Paul in 1 Corinthians 7:31.

> Seeing heaven and hell through God's eyes we under-
> stand how everything here on earth is like a play, a
> rehearsal for life up there. Play the part you will have up
> there (as Jesus would in your place, according to your
> vocation), and yours is a divine adventure that will be
> fulfilled and perpetuated up there. If you play your role
> poorly, doing what pleases you, then this false and lifeless
> scene will be perpetuated down there in the vanity of all
> things, to which you are attached.

We can better understand the depth of this affirmation if we keep in mind the way Chiara views the creation of all things and their return to the bosom of the Father. Here we can only briefly mention her understanding. We read in the famous Christological hymn at the beginning of the Letter to the Colossians, "All things were created through him [the Son] and for him" (Col 1:16). Chiara echoes the hymn when she writes:

> The Ideas of things were in the Word and the Father
> projected them outward.

She explains,

> I understood that in the act of creating, diverging rays
> came forth from the Father and that those rays gave order
> which is life, love and truth. . . . In the end, the Father will
> draw back those rays which, though previously divergent,
> will become convergent and meet in his bosom.

"On this side of heaven," that is, outside of the bosom of the Father, Chiara concludes, "there will be hell . . . matter without life, without order, without love."

Based on this fundamental vision of human beings and all creation we can understand Chiara's affirmation that what we live on earth will be perpetuated either in heaven or in hell. It depends on our response or lack of response to God's idea and, therefore, to the Word, which is our true being and which the Father has pronounced "from all eternity."

Consequently, no one will go to hell simply as a "punishment." We will be judged by our own actions, which in the presence of the Word will be revealed either as true and real or as false and lacking reality. The Fourth Gospel gives us perspective on this understanding: "If anyone hears my words and does not observe them, I do not condemn him, for I did not come to condemn the world but to save the world. Whoever rejects me and does not accept my words has something to judge him: the word that I spoke, it will condemn him on the last day" (Jn 12:47-48).[15]

As we can see, the perspective of Chiara Lubich is profoundly ontological. At the end of the world, when appearances pass away, we will see what *truly is*.

How are we to imagine hell?

In past centuries, according to the understanding of hell reached then by the collective consciousness, material and figurative representations (fire, various torments, etc.) played a big role when hell was discussed. Today, reflections on faith tend to affirm that we are speaking of a transcendent reality, one which goes beyond the categories of our senses.[16] Consequently the reality of hell is seen above all as a *state of being* rather than a place. "Fathers and teachers," exclaims Starets Sosima in *The Brothers Karamazov* by Dostoyevski, "I ask myself: 'What is hell?' I affirm that it is the torment of not being able to love."[17]

Jean Guitton affirms, "Our age, which does not believe in the afterlife and consequently does not believe in hell, has been able to describe the penalty due by using categories and new images that theologians have not employed. . . . The description of certain truly hellish states of human reality, due to feelings of anguish or guilt, vice, or even simple boredom with life, show how human persons, though they have reached such a high level of self-consciousness, nevertheless are eternally closed in themselves . . . through self torment and self torture."[18]

The vivid description given by Marcel Jouhandeau is significant in this light: "More visions of hell. Everything was gone, everything was suddenly at the end: air, light, but above all what made me despair was the certainty that I was relegated there forever in myself, without hope of anything, of nothing else, forever, neither to be able to leave, nor to receive visitors, nor to hear a sound, nor to be able to make the slightest movement . . . walled in, hermetically closed in a shell. . . . The memory of the anguish I experienced in that moment can never be erased, as if at other times I had not ever in any way been 'alone.' "[19]

Chiara speaks of hell very effectively and in a profoundly contemporary way. She writes,

> Everyone will be demented because they will all be alone and will talk to themselves. They will never be able to communicate with another and, if they do communicate, it will be to hurl insults that will increase the disunity. How terrible hell is!

In the light of a theology based on unity, hell is seen as the most complete "non-communion," "the frightful opposite of the communion of saints in the heavenly Jerusalem,"[20] whereas heaven is life and Trinitarian communion in the most complete sense imaginable. In heaven everyone, together and individually, will participate fully in the glory of God and, in him, in all of creation. To be excluded from such fullness of life is the greatest punishment, one much worse than physically burning in a sea of flames.[21]

In her concise and intuitive style, and on the basis of her fundamental understanding of hell as the opposite of

Trinitarian communion, Chiara expands further on hell as the anti-reality of heaven.

   a. *The perversion of all relationships.*
   In heaven, there exists perfect unity and perfect distinction, and therefore full communion and complete freedom at the same time. In hell this experience and interweaving of the Trinitarian life is blocked. She writes,

> And there will only be Unity without being Unity in the Trinity [that is, unity in variety], because only authority will exist. There will be Lucifer whom all will be forced to obey. In hell, there will be perfect unity and total anarchy, because no one will be wanting to do what they are doing, including Lucifer. Those who did not submit to authority here on earth, which would have made them free children of God, will be slaves for all eternity.

   Unlike heaven, in hell there will only be unity without freedom (i.e., coercion) and only freedom without unity (i.e., anarchy). Never, as we will see shortly, will there be the unity of opposites.

   b. *Time will be eternalized "in the negative."*
   Everything also has repercussions in the dimension of "temporality," if it can be expressed this way. "In eternity," Chiara Lubich explains referring to heaven,

> we will have a past, a present and a future, but these will be in unity. Everything will be concentrated in the present in which, besides experiencing its beatitude, there will also be remembrance (i.e., to give back to the heart, *ricordo*) of the past, which will not be remembrance but renewal, and the dream of the future, which will not be a dream but reality. As a result, eternity will never end because it is Trinitarian, and it will be all in the now because it is unitarian: the Eternal Present.

   In hell instead

time will be eternalized also, but with what a difference! Perennial will be not only the present infinite suffering but also the remembrance of the punishment already suffered and of the evil committed on earth and the expectation of the suffering to come in the future. The three sources of pain will be separate so that they will be increased and horribly confused among themselves.

Therefore:

Just as in heaven the honeymoon will be eternal and the mystical marriage with the Spouse will be repeated *ad infinitum*, so in hell one will go towards disunity *ad infinitum*.

And again:

In heaven, the more one enters in, the more unity and distinction will be accentuated. . . . In hell, the more one enters eternity the more division and confusion there will be . . . because, if heaven is Life Immortal, pure Act, hell is Immortal Death, only Death, constant dying.

c. *The "world" of the damned.*

Even though Chiara's understanding of hell has a strong existential value, it is not limited to the psychological level. It is an entire world, a cosmos of perversion.

People who on earth were attached to things that pass away . . . down there will find what is empty and vain and dead and painful and cold and fire, everything that inflicts hurt through burning or freezing, because cold (chattering of teeth) will never make unity with heat (eternal fire), which means it will never be tepid, since in hell two things will not be able to love one another. Everything will be there, but still and immobile. . . . There will also be people in motion, but without ever stopping. There will either be continuous movement or total stillness: never the unity of opposites, because unity would mean life.

Everything will be found down there, but disunited; shattered, without harmony, which is order.

Therefore, hell will be, as Chiara affirms with a very incisive image,

like a rigid corpse with every sign of life: eyes for seeing, an upper body to lift oneself up and breathe, a mouth for speaking, etc. Everything will be there but without a purpose.

Commenting on these insights, Chiara compares them to the experience of the "dark night" of the mystics, an extreme trial during which one no longer perceives God's presence and even comes to think that the physical world is "unreal."

The "dark night," as the mystics say, is truly an experience of hell. In hell the damned will see the sky with all the stars, and yet it will be all empty: it will be lacking the presence of God beneath all things. They will see everything as empty, without Love which is behind it all.

This resembles something we have already read:

On the other side of heaven there will remain hell. . . . It will remain as matter without life, without order, without love.

Therefore, Chiara affirms,

In hell, what will be will be empty illusion, unreality that the punished man will continue to see, not wanting to see it anymore, because he will then understand how empty and dead it is.

These affirmations offer us a strikingly incisive idea about hell, and yet at the same time they respect the biblical discretion concerning the modality of the life beyond. They place hell before us very effectively, as a situation of disunity, as the world of non-love. They therefore bring together the existential dimension to which the modern mentality is particularly sensitive, and the cosmic-objective dimension which is the classical concept of hell as a "place."

It is to be noted, and this too is in tune with modern thinking, that many of the characteristics of hell described in these passages can in some way be experienced here on earth. In hell, however, the rupture and the negation of relationship become irreversible, definitive. "Leave behind all hope, you who enter here," Dante had written about hell in *The Divine Comedy*.[22] And Chiara,

> Every part of this formless matter will hopelessly invoke the Form. It will have only one desire: to love. It is made to love, but it can no longer love. Actually matter will not have desires: it will seem to the damned that matter is "full of longing," as they are and will be for all eternity. In fact, the damned take their own immortal soul to hell with them. They will be fully aware that they should have done just one thing, to love, and that they cannot do it anymore. The "only one thing is necessary" will be their eternal torment.

Hell and Jesus forsaken

Reflecting on Chiara Lubich's thought in the perspective of unity, has brought new evidence and depth to the totally "negative" reality of hell. Consequently we are urged to commit ourselves with new determination to the way of love and unity which lies at the heart of the evangelical message.

Equally insightful is the other greatly significant point of the charism of unity—the mystery of Jesus crucified and forsaken. We will treat this topic at another time and in greater depth. Here we will limit ourselves to three briefly sketched points.

"Jesus forsaken," Chiara writes,

has drawn into himself everything that is vanity, and all that is vanity has become him, and he is God. There is no more emptiness on earth or in heaven: there is God.

Because of Jesus forsaken, therefore, hell has been conquered. In the next life there is no such thing as duality. Making himself disunity and even, as Paul says, "a curse" (Gal 3:13), "sin" (2 Cor 5:21) out of love for us, he has filled every emptiness with himself.

> By making himself sin . . . he became Nothingness. . . . Therefore, wherever the Father, and who is in him, sees nothingness, he sees Jesus forsaken, he sees himself: God. And therefore he sees God everywhere: heaven.

In Jesus forsaken, therefore, even hell has been brought back to the One. "All God, All Heaven, All Jesus," Chiara exclaims.

However, and here is our second consideration, this does not annul the greatness of man's freedom; man can reject God's gift forever. Hell, and therefore the perennial rejection of God, remains a real possibility. But how can this happen if only God *is,* if only Love *is?* Focusing on the heart of the mystery of the abandonment, Chiara discloses to us in this regard a perspective that is not so explicit in Christian thought.

> Jesus forsaken, who makes himself nothingness . . . has given reality to non-being, to hell too therefore, and to death. He has given life to death.

And therefore, because of Jesus forsaken, hell exists; but it exists as "the reality of unreality." It is unreality, because it is non-being, non-love, and therefore nothing. But Jesus forsaken makes it possible for this nothing to exist. Making himself nothingness, he makes non-being exist and gives life to death. Chiara thus concludes:

Therefore this death is there; it really exists, otherwise we would simply die and not exist anymore. . . . Instead there is a rising to eternal death (see Jn 5:29).

Can we hope, with Hans Urs von Balthasar, that such a tragic outcome of human freedom will not occur for anyone? Chiara does not answer this question, but she tells us clearly, and this is our third consideration, that even if we are sinners, as long as we are alive, we are never hopelessly lost. If in the experience of the abandonment Jesus descended into the most profound darkness of sin, no one is so far from God that Jesus cannot reach him, so to speak, from within. Therefore, no matter what moral situation one might be in, in Jesus everyone can find a direct road to God. "Since Jesus made himself sin and therefore disunity," Chiara writes,

> he, as the abandoned one, can be the spouse even of the greatest sinner in the world, even when separated from everyone. Because he, as sin, identifies with every sinner, and every sinner can identify with him.

Here is our big opportunity, the Good News: it is enough that, with a pure act of love, we identify ourselves with him. "Whoever is in the Father," Chiara writes,

> coming from a long life of sin, is, in God's eyes, through God's mercy, just like the innocent one who got there through an ardent love.
> In fact, the moment one recognizes oneself as a sinner and (loving God more than one's own soul, which is pure love) rejoices at being similar to him who became sin, one fills all the emptiness created by sin.
> Thus one reaches heaven purely through God's mercy (receiving everything gratuitously) but at the same time through pure love of God freely expressed from one's heart.

Chiara Lubich affirms that Jesus forsaken "is the key to everything." And, truthfully, what matters in the end is not speculations about an "empty" hell, but the extraordinary possibility offered to us in Jesus to be saved from it and to have life. "Therefore, stay awake," he said, "for you know neither the day nor the hour" (Mt 25:13).

Hubertus Blaumeiser

Notes

1. Jean-Paul Sartre, *No Exit and Three Other Plays*, New York 1955, p. 95.

2. See J. Guitton according to whom "the damned manifest the sacred and dramatic character of this existence of ours" ("L'inferno e la mentalitá contemporanea," in G. Bardy and others, *L'Inferno*, Brescia 1953, 242). E.J. Ratzinger: "The dogma on hell does not merely supply us with information on the afterlife, rather it tells us kerygmatically something about our current life, something that has to do with our here and now." Therefore the message of the dogma on hell is "to bring people to lead their lives aware of the real possibility of an eternal failure and of understanding revelation as an extremely serious entreaty" (*Lexikon für Theologie und Kirche*, vol. 5, Freiburg i. Br. 1960, p. 448) (own translation).

3. *L'inferno e la mentalitá contemporanea*, pp. 231-232.

4. See what has been collected by H. U. von Balthasar in: *Breve discorso sull'inferno*, Brescia 1993, pp. 29-32.

5. See *Was dürfen wir hoffen?*, Einsiedeln 1986.

6. See *Breve discorso sull'inferno*, p. 33. See also John Paul II, *Crossing the Threshold of Hope*, New York 1994, p. 185, who, however, expresses himself with greater caution.

7. Cited by J. Guitton in *L'inferno e la mentalitá contemporanea*, p. 246. Note, however, that Guitton says, "We cannot know in what measure such a possibility happened to people. We know instead through faith that many spiritual creatures did not escape this misfortune" (p. 228) (own translation).

8. *Crossing the Threshold of Hope*, pp. 179ff. Similar perspectives can also be found in the Fathers of the Church.

9. See *L'Avvenire*, March 16, 1996.

10. See, among others, J. Moltmann, *Umkehr zur Zukunft*, Munich 1970, p. 80.

11. A. David-Neel, *Le bouddisme*, p. 177; cited by M. Carrouges, "Immagini dell'inferno nella letteratura," in G. Bardy and others, *L'inferno*, p. 47.

12. From: *Del male e della libertá* in J. Guitton, *L'inferno e la mentalitá contemporanea*, p. 247.

13. *Immagini dell'inferno nella letteratura*, p. 50.

14. *L'inferno*, p. 39.

15. See also John 3:19-21: "And this is the verdict, that the light came into the world, but people preferred darkness to light because their works were evil. For everyone who does wicked things hates the light and does not come toward the light, so that his works might not be exposed. But whoever lives the truth comes to the light, so that his works may be clearly seen as done in God."

16. We find in the Fathers of the Church a reflection on how the "fire" of hell of which Jesus spoke should be understood. The explanations waver between a physical fire (some even held that the true and personal hell could begin only after the universal judgment because to suffer in hell one needs a body; the Church later decided differently on this) and spiritual fire (see *Lexikon für Theologie und Kirche*, vol. 5, pp. 446-448; *Dizionario patristico e di antichitá cristiane*, vol. 2, Rome 1984, pp. 1775-78).

17. This is not a new idea. Origen had already interpreted hell as the inner torment of the conscience. Among those who held this viewpoint was Martin Luther. "I also know a man," he declared, in an autobiographical witness recalling the words of Paul in 2 Cor 12:2, "who was sure to have experienced these pains; they lasted only a short time but they were many and so hellish that no tongue could speak of them, no pen could describe them, and no one who hadn't experienced them could believe it. . . . God, and all creation with him, seemed to be terribly angry. There one has no way out, nor is there any consolation, neither inside nor outside, rather everything is transformed into accuser" (*Resolutiones circa le 95 tesi sull'indulgenza* (1518), WA 1, pp. 557ff.) (own translation).

18. *L'inferno e la mentalitá contemporanea*, p. 237. In this regard see K. Rahner: "This person closed off in his own solitude, who exists now only in himself because he did not want anything but himself, now wanders, so to speak, within the darkness of his own being, transformed into a prison, without ever coming out of it. He is restricted to an eternal monologue" (*Betrachtungen zum ignatianischen Exerzitienbuch*, Munich 1965, pp. 94ff.). E. J. Ratzinger sees the core of hell "in the loss of the being-in the Eternal Love, in definitively missing it and finding oneself in emptiness and self enclosure." This does not exclude the fact that hell has a cosmic-objective dimension as well. "The being-with of the world . . . becomes torment" (*Lexikon für Theologie und Kirche*, vol. 5, p. 449) (own translations).

19. *Essai sur moi-même*, p. 204; in M. Carrouges, *Immagini dell'inferno nella letteratura*, p. 52.

20. M. Carrouges, *L'inferno*, p. 56.

21. Cf. John Chrystosom: "I maintain that not to reach glory is far worse than to live in hell, and whoever falls from up there, does not so much suffer for the evils of hell as much as for the loss of the kingdom of heaven. Indeed this is the worst reproach" (*Letter to Theodore*, 12) (own translation).

22. *The Divine Comedy*, Canticle III, v. 9.

A Few Notes On Jesus Forsaken

Giuseppe Zanghi, editor-in-chief of the Nuova Umanità *review, is a philosopher and part of the initial core of the Abba School. His article is centered on Jesus forsaken, a key element of the spirituality of the Focolare and an essential component in Chiara's writings of 1949.*

Paul reveals to us that in Jesus "are hidden all the treasures of wisdom and knowledge" (Col 2:3), because Jesus is "the mystery of God" (Col 2:2) completely manifested to the world.

And the fullness of the manifestation is offered to us, according to Paul, by Jesus crucified: for this reason, the Apostle wants to know him alone (cf. 1 Cor 2:2). And for this reason, continues Paul, "I even consider everything as a loss because of the supreme good of knowing Christ Jesus my Lord. For his sake I have accepted the loss" of all things that are not him "and I consider them so much rubbish" (Phil 3:8).

The thirst for truth—which is also the thirst for beauty and goodness—which every person keeps in his or her heart and which is the person's very authenticity, can be quenched only by drinking from the mystery of Jesus, and of Jesus crucified. By drinking this water—which is the Holy Spirit—every person who draws near it is transformed into a spring of living water (cf. Jn 7:38).

Paul, therefore, wants to know and announce only Jesus and Jesus crucified.

Chiara Lubich proceeds along the way indicated by Paul, penetrating into the depths of his words and opening new expanses of human-divine light. I think in fact that only the same Spirit who put into Paul's heart the words he says to us could have revealed this to Chiara: in the crucifixion of Jesus it is in the mysterious wound of his abandonment, at the apex of his suffering and annihilation, that Jesus is fully himself.
Chiara writes,

> Jesus is Jesus forsaken [because Jesus is totally revealed in his abandonment]. Jesus forsaken is Jesus [that is, the true Jesus is Jesus forsaken].

And with a statement that penetrates into the essence of the Christian faith, Chiara concludes,

> Which is like saying: Being is Love.

In fact, Love, as Chiara continually says in the light of Jesus forsaken, is nothing other than Being in its truest identity. Love, as it is revealed in the Trinity, is Being completely given in the dynamics of the Divine Persons. But since these dynamics are perfect communion in that atemporal instant that is eternity, we need to conclude that Being absolutely *is*. Giving, in fact, truly means stripping oneself of something in order to give it to another. Now, what can Being be stripped of if not itself? However, since this stripping takes place in the reciprocity of the Three in that atemporal instant which is eternity, it is Being itself in its infinite timeliness.
In God, One and Triune, then, Being and Non-Being express the reality of Love, without being confused one with the other, but being one in the other. Love, as Chiara presents it to us, is the ultimate word that we can say about God because he himself revealed it, that word which the human mind has always searched for and could not find.

Jesus forsaken, Chiara continues, is

> the miracle of the annihilation of that which is. A miracle that can be understood only by those who know Love and who know that in Love all and nothing coincide.

It is the intimate life of God. In fact,

> if we consider the Word in the Father, we think of the Word as nothing [the nothing of Love] so as to think of God as One. If we consider the Father in the Word we think of the Father as nothing [the nothing of Love].

We can say that the Three Persons

> are one because Love is and is not at the same time but it also *is* when it *is not* because it is Love. In fact, if I take something from myself and I give it [I deprive myself—it is not] out of love, I have love [it is].

In this light Chiara writes,

> Jesus is Jesus forsaken. Because Jesus is the Savior, the Redeemer, and he redeems when he pours the Divine onto humanity through the wound of the abandonment.

The words of Chiara we just read open to our intelligence a new way. A new knowledge takes shape in all fields: theology, art, science. And we are invited to use a language which, while reaching the truth in its most profound depths, can express it with divine simplicity.

On the other hand, if Jesus forsaken is all this, we can easily understand that nothing we say can ever express him completely. Jesus forsaken is an inexhaustible richness of a thousand faces, a thousand nuances, which only wisdom—the wisdom that God gives us (and in the measure that we live it)—can grasp in a global way. In fact, the richness which is Jesus forsaken is, in view of what we said on being and non-being, the highest poverty—that poverty which, in this light, means perfect unity. Reflections, studies, can grasp one aspect of Jesus forsaken or another. We need to take care never to stop at any level reached, but rather to allow ourselves always and continually to be taken up by the pure light of unity in order to return to our studies, perhaps with a greater capacity to understand, and once again and always to know how to let go of these studies in the face of that something more which is wisdom.

In this brief conversation I will say something about one aspect of Jesus forsaken.

In view of what I have said so far, we can say that Jesus in the abandonment unifies two nothings: the Nothing that is Love because it is Trinity, and the nothing that is created being. In reality, created being as such, in itself, is nothing: a nothing, however, that should also have been a nothing-love, therefore, a *being*, in giving itself back to God (and, we add, neighbors) if sin had not fixed and closed it into itself, making of it a negative nothing: a closure, a turning in on self, a rejection of others. In his abandonment Jesus made this negative nothing his own, turning it back into the positive Nothing which is Love; that is, drawing it back into God's plan.

Chiara writes,

> In his cry Jesus forsaken has summed up the nothingness of things: "All things are vanity" (Qo 1:2).

But by doing so, he gave divine consistency to all things.

> Jesus forsaken is the vanity, and he is the Word; he is that which passes and that which remains, because he is the God-man. As man, he is all that is created which is vanity of vanities; as God, he is the fire that consumes in itself all things, the nothing.

But, Chiara specifies,

> . . . divinizing it. Jesus forsaken breathed in all vanities, and vanities became him, and he is God.

The nothing of what is created is introduced into the Nothing-Love of the life of the Trinity and, therefore, is led into Being, which is Love, and that is to *really* be.

Chiara continues,

> In making himself nothing, Jesus forsaken also remains everything, because he is all Love, God Being, Pure Love. Non-Being clothed with Love.

That is, we still remain created beings, but we are all clothed with the Being of God, which is Love. For this reason, life in Christ knows no sunset; the meaning of death changes.

In Jesus forsaken we are introduced into the heart of God Love. That Love urged the Father to give us the Son and the Son to give us the Father in the way that they give themselves in the Trinity, thus taking us up into their life.

But in order to truly give us the Father, the Son, *in his humanity*, necessarily had to experience the lacerating sensation of losing him, because the creature (and the humanity of Jesus is creature) is in time and space—intervals that need to be crossed in order to encounter God and other created beings; whereas in eternity, which is God, the encounter of the Three is both their distinction and their unity. But it is to this very reality that Jesus forsaken introduces the creature, with his humanity, and with us in it. For this reason Jesus loses God for us, making his humanity—as Chiara says—live that which he, God in God, lives in the glory of his divinity.

Jesus, writes Chiara,

> gave God and found God again in himself [in his humanity] and in everyone.

And here we have a point of great relevance that I would like to offer for your reflection.

The divine Person of the Word, in order to make of us God, reaches down to us in the deepest part of our humanity, making himself, as Chiara says, "individuality." Chiara tells us that Jesus, "having made himself sin, is reduced to being a mere man, to being 'individuality,' no longer *the* man" in his full universality, as Adam was called to be (and partially he was) before the fall, and as Jesus was in the Incarnation. He, who was *the* man *par excellence* because he is the Son of God, made himself "one of many men." On the other hand, Jesus is God and he remains *the* man *par excellence*, the One. His descending all the way to the limits of the created beings closed in their individuality meant this: for Jesus, the abandonment (which he overcame in love); for us, to be taken up by him, so as to receive as a gift his reality as Son of God. *It meant receiving as a gift that reality of personhood* that was given to us in the earthly paradise by vocation—because we were created in the image of God—a vocation obscured in Adam but regained for us in Jesus, and brought to fulfillment if we allow ourselves to be made one by him and in him.

Chiara tells us here in a very profound way what it means for each one of us to be person. She writes:

> I have always been in the mind of God, in the Word, and I have always been loved by the Father. Therein lies my true self: Christ in me.

My life's story is to allow myself to be led by Jesus, who comes to take me there where I am, as a created being and a sinner, and to lead me into my true reality, which I have always been in the mind of God but which I must become by doing my part. We have here again that being and non-being that distinguishes all of Chiara's thought. She explains:

> God's idea of a person is God. It is a matter of the place that Jesus has prepared: our place is the thought he has of us, and we go to occupy it. My personality, in fact, is Christ in me, which is very different from the Christ in Saint Catherine, from the Christ in Saint Francis, from the Christ in any other person. By losing *our* human personality, we acquire that of Christ, one which is much stronger, much more distinct from others. But we must

have the courage to lose *our* personality, whereas today everyone wants to assert it.

And now I would like to quote a great theologian of the Eastern Church, Sergio Bulgakov: "Adam, before the sin, although he was a specific person, a concrete *self*, possessed in himself the fullness of humanity; he was the *total man* in whom there lived the whole human race with every possible personality. In this sense, Adam, though a person, did not have individuality in the negative, limiting meaning of this word, a result of dispersed unity which became the bad multiplicity of self-centeredness. Our fallen humanity understands personality as individual. We have no other knowledge of individuality, and we are proud of it, as of the only form of personality available to us. But it wasn't like this in the beginning, in the wisdom-filled image of man wherein the personality must be transparent: . . . everything in everyone, and each one in all; this is the ontology of the personality. In Adam, because of sin, the image of the total humanity was obscured; he became a mere individuality which could only generate other individualities. And the first of those generated by Adam was Cain, in whom self-centeredness appeared in all its power, to the point of fratricide. Cain, together with all the little Cains who followed, was the first individualist. Such individuality is linked to the sin of the origins, with the loss of the wisdom-filled image of man. But in the New Adam (Jesus) this wisdom-filled image of man is fulfilled and the bad individuality is overcome ("I do not seek my own will, but the will of the Father who sent me"; "Whoever wishes to come after me, must deny himself"; these are the principles of the new life in Christ)."[1]

And here my destiny as a human being is at stake. Jesus in the abandonment has revealed to me that one is by not being, because this is Love, this is the life of God. So then, the gift that God gives to me of my personhood is something that I must give back to him by *losing it in order to receive it again from him*, but now, through Jesus, within God himself. As creatures in Jesus, we live the life that the Father and the Son live; Jesus makes himself one with us to the very abyss of our individuality, even to sin: that individuality which we were supposed to live—and we should live—like the dawn of the person we are called to be but which the sin of Adam has blocked, has led to being turned in on itself. Jesus brings to full bloom in his divine person the individual he reached in his abandonment; and he calls all of us to blossom as persons in the Word, coming out of ourselves in him in order to truly be ourselves in him. The dawn of the Garden of Eden, now in Jesus, reaches its highest point in the midday sun.

This is the reality offered to us here on earth right now. Jesus forsaken tells us precisely this, providing that we enter into his logic and we live like him.

I would like to conclude with a passage written by Chiara in which we are told what we can be if we are a living Jesus forsaken.

> Jesus forsaken, because he is not, he is [Chiara adds: "because he loves he is"].
> We are if we are not. If we are, we are not.
> We must be "thought-free" because we are children of God. The children of God do not have thoughts. Only when we do not have thoughts will our mind be completely open and constantly receive the light of God and be a channel. [Chiara adds, "We are asked to be detached from our way of thinking, from thinking itself: this is the non-being of the mind. This is what makes us like Jesus forsaken, and this holds true also for the will, the memory and the imagination."]
> Likewise, we must be without will [our will in the possessive sense of the word] in order to have the capacity of the will of God.
> We must be without memory in order to remember only the present moment and live "ecstatically" [outside ourselves].
> We must be without imagination in order to see Paradise

also with our imagination because Paradise is the Dream of dreams.

Giuseppe M. Zanghi

Notes

1. *L'agnello di Dio*, Rome, 1986, p. 265.

The Resurrection of Rome

The reading together of Chiara's texts which record the intuitions she had in the experience of 1949 form the cornerstone of the Abba School's work. Three brief portions of Chiara's texts that have been already published are included here. The Resurrection of Rome, *revised by the author, was published in the periodical La Via 36 (1949), a magazine edited by Igino Giordani. This text is followed by* Look At All the Flowers *and* Give Me Everyone Who Is Lonely. *All these reflect the depth of content and also the richness of form of the entire corpus of notes of 1949-1950.*

If I look at this city of Rome, as it is, I feel my Ideal is very far away, as far as ancient times when great saints and great martyrs shed rays of eternal light upon the world around them, even upon the walls of monuments that still stand and bear witness to the love that united the early Christians.

What incredible contrast to the vain and soiled worldliness that now dominates the streets and, to an even greater extent, the homes where anger and every other kind of sin and disturbance lurk in every corner.

I would call my Ideal a utopia if I didn't think of the One who saw such a world around him too and who, at the height of his life, seemed overwhelmed by it, as though evil had defeated him.

He, too, looked out upon a great crowd of people whom he loved as he loved himself. He who created the world would have wanted to extend the bonds that were to unite all people to himself as children to their Father, and as brothers and sisters to one another.

He had come to bring the family back together—to make all people one.

Yet, in spite of his words of Fire and Truth that could burn off the vanities that smother the Eternal within and among the people, many people, though they comprehended his words, didn't want to understand. Their darkened souls left them blind.

He created them with the power of free will.

He who had come down from heaven could have brought everyone back to life with just a glance alone. But he had to leave it up to them, created as they were in God's image and likeness, to discover the joy of the free conquest of heaven. Eternity was at stake, and for all Eternity they could live like children of God, like God, creators of their own happiness (thanks to their participation in the almighty power of God).

He looked at the world just as I see it, but he didn't doubt. As he prayed at night, dissatisfied and saddened for a world headed for ruin, he turned his glance again to heaven above and to heaven within him. There dwelled the Trinity, the true Being, the Everything that was real, while outside on the streets the nothingness that passes away still wandered aimlessly about.

In order to believe in the final victory of Light over darkness, in order to remain connected to the Eternal, to the Uncreated, root of the created, and therefore, the Life of everything, I do the same as he.

I go through Rome, not wanting to look at it. I look instead at the world within me; I hold on to what has meaning and value. I make myself completely one with the Trinity who resides in my soul, and who enlightens my soul with eternal light, filling it with all of heaven populated by the angels and saints who, too . . . can be found in my small person recollected with the Three in a unity of love, for they are not subject to space and time.

And I encounter the Fire that invades the humanity God gave me and makes me another Christ, another God-man by participation. My humanity merges with the divine. My eyes are no longer closed. In fact, it is through the pupil of my eye, the empty channel to my soul which allows all the light that is within me to pass (if I allow God to live in me) that I look at the world and everything in it. But it is no longer I who look. It is Christ in me who looks and sees once again the blind to enlighten, the mute to be given voice, and the crippled to heal. They are blind to the vision of God within and outside of themselves; deaf to the word of God who speaks in them as well, and through whom the truth can be awakened in others; crippled because they have become immobilized, ignorant of the divine will that in the depths of their hearts spurs them to eternal movement, to eternal love, through which one becomes inflamed by spreading its fire.

In this way, I open my eyes to what is outside of myself, and I see humanity with the eyes of God, who is all-trusting because he is love.

I see and discover my own Light, my true Reality, my true self (buried perhaps or secretly camouflaged out of shame) in the others. Having found myself again, I unite myself to myself [in them], reviving myself—as Love which is Life—in my neighbors.

In this way, I revive Jesus in them, another Christ, another God-man, the manifestation of the Father's goodness here on earth, the eyes of God on humanity. Thus, I extend the Christ in me to my neighbor; I form a living and complete cell of the mystical body of Christ, a living cell, a hearth of God possessing the Fire that is to be communicated, along with the Light, to others.

From two, God makes one by placing himself as third, as the relationship between them: Jesus among us.

In this way love, through its inherent law of communion, circulates like a river of fire, and naturally carries along with it all that the two possess in order to achieve a communion of both material and spiritual goods.

This bears active and visible witness to unifying love, true love, the love of the Trinity. Then the total Christ truly relives in both, in each one, and among us.

It is Christ, God-man, with the most diversified expressions of the human imbued with the divine which are placed at the service of the eternal goal: God whose interest is the kingdom; it is he, an impartial Father, who is the ruler of all, the giver of every good to all his children.

* * *

And I think that by allowing God to live in me, and by letting him love himself in my neighbors, he would discover himself in many. Many eyes would then shine with his light, giving a tangible sign that he reigns there.

And the Fire purifying all things, at the service of Eternal Love, would spread quickly throughout Rome to bring Christians back from the dead and transform this so-called atheistic era, into an era of Fire, an era of God.

But in the effort to bring back some Christianity, we need to have the courage not to consider other means which would only re-echo past glories; or at least we should not overestimate these means.

The point is that we need to bring God back to life in us, then keep him alive, and therefore overflow him onto others like bursts of Life that revive the dead.

And we need to keep him alive among us by loving one another (and to love one another doesn't require a lot of noise: love means death to ourselves—death is silence—and life in God—and God is silence that speaks).

Then everything changes, politics and art, education and religion, private life and recreation. Everything.

God is not in us like a crucifix hanging on a classroom wall.
He is alive in us if we let him live, and he gives order to every
human and divine law because everything comes from him.
And from within us he, the eternal teacher, speaks, teaching
the eternal and the temporal, giving value to everything.

But we cannot understand this unless we let him live in us
by living in others, because life is love and if love doesn't circu-
late it doesn't live.

Jesus must see his Resurrection in the Eternal City and be
made present everywhere. He is Life, complete Life. And not
only in the religious realm.[1] To separate him from the total life
of a person is a practical heresy of our times. It enslaves people
to something which is beneath them, relegating God, who is
Father, somewhere far from his children.[2]

---

1. At times there is a tendency to think that the Gospel cannot solve
    every human problem but is intended to bring about the kingdom of
    God understood only in a religious sense. But it is not so. It is
    certainly not the historical Jesus or he, as the head of the mystical
    body, who resolves all the problems. This is done by Jesus in us,
    Jesus in me, Jesus in you. . . . It is Jesus in that person, in that given
    person—when his grace lives in that person—who builds a bridge,
    who opens a way. Jesus is the true, most profound personality of
    every person. Every human being (every Christian) is, in fact, more
    a child of God (another Jesus) than a child of one's own father.
    Every person gives his or her particular contribution to all human
    fields as another Christ, as a member of his mystical body, whether
    it is in politics, science, or art. . . . This is the continuation of the
    Incarnation, the complete Incarnation which concerns every Jesus
    of the mystical body of Christ.
2. The human person, in all his or her dimensions and capabilities, is
    not to be lowered but elevated. Besides a "new," renewed theology
    (based on the Trinitarian life lived in the mystical body of Christ),
    there is need for a new science, a new sociology, a new art, new
    politics: new because they are of Christ, renewed by his Spirit.
    There is need to open up a new humanism where the the human
    person is truly at the center, the human person who is above all
    Christ, Christ in people.

No, he is *the* man, the perfect person, summarizing in himself all people, all truth and every impulse that they might have to elevate themselves to their rightful place.

And he who has found Christ, this Man, has found the solution to every problem, whether human or divine. It is enough to love him.

Chiara Lubich

Look At All the Flowers

People who are aiming at perfection generally try to be united with God in their own hearts.

It is as if they were standing in a large garden full of flowers and they look at and admire only one flower. They look at it with love, in every detail and as a whole, but they don't pay much attention to the other flowers.

God, through the collective spirituality he has given us, is asking us to look at all the flowers (our brothers and sisters) because he is in all of them, and only by observing them all do we love him more than the individual flowers. God who is in me, who has shaped my soul, who dwells in it as Trinity, is also in my neighbor's heart. . . . And just as I love Him in myself, recollecting myself in Him when I am alone, so too I love Him in my neighbor when he or she is beside me. Thus I will not only love silence but the word, that is, the communication of God in me with God in my brother. . . .

Yes, it is necessary to recollect oneself also in the presence of our brothers or sisters too but without fleeing from them, rather recollecting them in my Heaven and recollecting myself in their Heaven. And since this Trinity is in human bodies, Jesus, the Man-God, is there. And between the two there is unity in which we are one but not alone. And here is the miracle of the Trinity and the beauty of God who is not alone because He is Love.

Therefore, when the soul has willingly lost the God within itself all day long so as to transfer itself into the God in the other (because one is the same as the other, just as the two flowers in that garden are the work of the same Creator), when it has done this for love of Jesus forsaken, who leaves God for God (and precisely God in one "soul" for the God who is present or is being born in the brother...), the soul re-entering itself or rather God in itself (because it is now alone in prayer or meditation) will rediscover the caress of the Spirit who, being Love, is truly Love because God cannot but fulfill His word and give to whoever has given. He gives Love to whoever has loved.

So darkness and unhappiness along with aridity and all bitter things vanish, and only the full joy promised to those who have lived unity remains. The cycle is complete. We have to seek continuously to give life to these living cells of the mystical body of Christ, which are our brothers and sisters united in His name, so as to breathe life into the whole body. . . ."

Chiara Lubich

Give Me Everyone Who Is Lonely

Lord, give me everyone who is lonely.
I feel in my heart the passion that fills your heart
    for the forsakenness enveloping the whole world.
I love everyone who is sick and lonely:
I even feel for plants that are in distress,
    and for animals that are left alone.
Who will console their weeping?
Who will feel compassion for their slow death?
Who will press a heart in despair to one's own heart?
Let me be in this world, my God, the tangible
    sacrament of your love, of your being Love:
Let me be your arms to embrace and transform
    into love all the loneliness of the world.

Chiara Lubich

THE CRY
of Jesus Crucified and Forsaken
by Chiara Lubich
with a Foreword by Cardinal Paul Poupard

"*The Cry* provides a glimpse into the formation, trials, and spirituality of the Focolare Movement. Each page is filled with intensely spiritual insights about the forsaken Savior, on whom members of the Movement model their lives. . . . Lubich writes as one so consumed with love that she cannot help but share her joy. Her style is poetic and her message brief but interwoven with mystery. It is only through uniting ourselves entirely with the forsaken Christ that suffering finds meaning, and joy becomes possible."

New Oxford Review

ISBN 1-56548-159-3, 2d printing, 5 1/8 x 8, 128 pp.

JESUS: THE HEART OF HIS MESSAGE
Unity and Jesus Forsaken
by Chiara Lubich

"Without being simplistic or reductionistic, Lubich challenges her associates to focus on Jesus forsaken as the model for unity and the key to living a life of joy."

Bishop Robert F. Morneau

ISBN 1-56548-090-2, 2d printing, paper, 5 1/8 x 8, 112 pp.

A CALL TO LOVE
Spiritual Writings, vol. 1

by Chiara Lubich

"Chiara Lubich has established herself as a Christian writer of considerable proportions. Given her prolific literary output it is fitting that New City Press should issue a retrospective series of Lubich's best works, titled Spiritual Writings. The first work in this series *A Call to Love* comprises three of her most popular studies of momentous Christian living: *Our Yes to God* (1980), *The Word of Life* (1974), and *The Eucharist* (1977)."

B.C. Catholic

ISBN 1-56548-077-5, 2d printing, 5 1/8 x 8, 180 pp.

WHEN OUR LOVE IS CHARITY
Spiritual Writings, vol. 2

by Chiara Lubich

"The author draws on some of the best elements of the Catholic tradition to speak a credible word for the world today. The text actually is a compilation of three independent works with the first being the book's title. The other two sections are *Jesus in Our Midst* and *When Did We See You Lord?*"

The Cord

ISBN 0-911782-93-1, 2d printing, paper, 5 1/8 x 8, 152 pp.

CHRISTIAN LIVING TODAY
Meditations
by Chiara Lubich

"Like shafts of sunlight that break through the clouds on a dreary day, these meditations touch us and turn our most mundane activities into brightly lit God-moments."

Liguorian

ISBN 1-56548 -094-5, 7th printing, paper 5 1/8 x 8, 158 pp.

HEAVEN ON EARTH
Meditations and Reflections
by Chiara Lubich

Heaven on Earth is an inspiring collection of reflections spanning the past fifty years of Chiara Lubich's writing. This beautiful medley of meditations, all newly translated and many available for the first time in English, provides a striking, panoramic view of her gospel-based spirituality, centered around Jesus' last testament, "Father, may they all be one" (Jn 17:21).

"In these pages we are invited to drink from the spiritual sources which have nourished her own life and the lives of millions of others."

Michael Downey

ISBN 1-56548-144-5, paper, 5 1/8 x 8, 176 pp.

HERE AND NOW
Meditations on Living in the Present
by Chiara Lubich

Thought-provoking reflections to help us grasp and shape the "here and now" as God's gift to us.

"Chiara Lubich's *Here and Now* meditations have the unifying theme of the meaning of time, the present moment, in our spiritual journey. Our own time is limited, but the present moment is the way to be connected with what is unlimited and outside of time: eternity."

Catholic Library World

ISBN 1-56548-138-0, hardcover, 5 3/8 x 8, 64 pp.

ONLY AT NIGHT WE SEE THE STARS
Finding Light in the Face of Darkness
by Chiara Lubich
with a Foreword by Bishop Robert F. Morneau

"For those who are yearning for spiritual growth and insight into God's word and the meaning of human existence, these prayer-filled reflections by Chiara Lubich will be most helpful.... This is not a book to be read. It is a spiritual manual to be prayed and pondered. Here is a wine which, if sipped slowly and lovingly, will lead to divine intoxication. It will also call us to the justice and peace that characterizes the followers of Jesus" (from the Foreword).

ISBN 1-56548-1158-5, hardcover, 5 3/8 x 8, 88 pp.

Also Available from New City Press

MAY THEY ALL BE ONE
by Chiara Lubich

The author tells her story and that of the Focolare Movement. The perfect book for those who wish to know more about the Focolare and the spirituality of unity.

ISBN 0-911782-46-X, 7th printing, paper, 4 1/2 x 7, 92 pp.

JOURNEY TO HEAVEN
Spiritual Thoughts to Live
by Chiara Lubich

This is the third volume of Chiara's spiritual thoughts given in monthly conference calls. It is not only inspirational but it is a practical reference guide on how to live heavenly realities in our everyday lives.
ISBN 1-56548-093-7, paper, 5 1/8 x 8, 146 pp.

A LIFE FOR UNITY
An Interview with Chiara Lubich
by Franca Zambonini

"This little book's 175 pages of text are a fast and intriguing read. The insights are uplifting and Chiara's delight in a gospel that is still new and fresh after 2,000 years is contagious. She confirms that Christians are still known by their love for one another."

Catholic Advocate

ISBN 0-904287-45-9, 2d printing, paper, 5 1/8 x 8, 181 pp.